some words of Myshkin'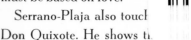
only just, is unjust"—implyi
must be based on love.

Serrano-Plaja also touch
Don Quixote. He shows t
man of flesh and blood, stirred by the physical
attractions of women, and not just the sexless
platonic lover he is usually made out to be.

According to Serrano-Plaja's theory, the
game continues until Don Quixote's final
defeat and his approaching death. With a
final, private wink at Sancho, the Knight lets
us know that the "game" is still being played.
Serrano-Plaja's new theory of the *Quixote* is
so appealing that we accept it with pleasure,
feeling that we are participants in the eternal
game that Don Quixote and Sancho play.

Professor Serrano-Plaja's *Realismo
"mágico" en Cervantes* was first published in
Madrid (Editorial Gredos, 1967).

Arturo Serrano-Plaja, Professor of Spanish
at the University of California, Santa Bar-
bara, is the author of numerous volumes of
prose and poetry, and a prolific translator. His
poetry has appeared in many anthologies, including Kenneth Rexroth's *Thirty Spanish
Poems of Love and Exile*. In his introduction
he credits the seed for his present study to an
encounter with Ernest Hemingway during the
Spanish Civil War: "So that afternoon I
learned about two things from the Anglo-
Saxon world: whiskey and the importance of
Mark Twain."

"MAGIC" REALISM
IN CERVANTES

"MAGIC" REALISM IN CERVANTES

Don Quixote as Seen Through Tom Sawyer and The Idiot

Arturo Serrano-Plaja

Translated by Robert S. Rudder

UNIVERSITY OF CALIFORNIA PRESS
BERKELEY, LOS ANGELES, AND LONDON · 1970

University of California Press
Berkeley and Los Angeles, California

University of California Press, Ltd.
London, England

First published in Spanish
by Editoral Gredos, S. A., Madrid, Spain,
under the title *Realismo "mágico" en Cervantes:*
"Don Quijote" visto desde "Tom Sawyer" y "El Idiota"
(© Arturo Serrano-Plaja, 1967).

SBN: 520-01591-6
Library of Congress Catalog Card Number: 71-94991

Designed by Dave Comstock
Printed in the United States of America

Translator's Note

Following the original edition in Spanish, a bibliography of works consulted for this study is given at the end, to which all page numbers cited in the text refer. For detailed quotations from the works of Cervantes and Dostoevski, the translations of Walter Starkie and Constance Garnett, respectively, have been used. In a few cases the translations have been altered slightly, when a more literal interpretation seemed necessary.

Finally, some words of indebtedness to various people must be expressed. First, to Miss Constance Sullivan for her diligent reading and many helpful suggestions when this translation was no more than a rough draft. Second, to my wife, Karen, for her help in the final readings and typing. And, finally, to my friend, the author of this work—Arturo Serrano-Plaja—for his confidence.

Robert S. Rudder

Contents

Introduction

Let us be honest about it: the *Quixote* is an ambiguity. All the exaggerated praise coming from our country has been useless. All the scholarly research on Cervantes has not cleared up even the most minute part of this monumental ambiguity. Is Cervantes making fun? And what is he making fun of? From a distance, alone in the open Manchegan plains, the long figure of Don Quixote bends like an interrogation mark, like a guardian of the Spanish secret, of the ambiguity of Spanish culture. This poor tax collector, from the depths of a jail cell: what is he mocking? And just what does it mean to mock? [P. 46]
Ortega y Gasset, *Meditations on the Quixote*

During our Civil War in Spain I had the opportunity to meet Ernest Hemingway, for whose writing in general I have great respect. And I have a very profound admiration for some particular works of his. I must have talked with him about seven or eight times altogether, but five or six of them were simply everyday conversations. I only remember talking with him seriously twice. Once—the last time—was in the Majestic Hotel in Barcelona, and it turned into an argument:

Even Hemingway wanted to denounce me because I had taken Waldo Frank to visit the front lines and had introduced him to the Commander of the Army of the Ebro, the unit I was with during the last stages of the war.

Hemingway, speaking a jargon that was supposed to be Spanish "slang," said many things to me: he insinuated that I was an "enemy of the people"; he asserted that Waldo Frank was a "Trotskyite"—a label that in those times and circumstances could bring about the gravest of consequences; and to muster all the indignation he felt for my conduct, he used a very Spanish phrase, if ever there was one: "You have ba——s!" But instead of using the verb "to have," he seized (if I may use the expression) the verb "to be," and the phrase came out quite picturesquely: "You are ba——s!" [1] Later, when I saw the title of one of his novels, which was apparently reminiscent of Shakespeare, *To Have and to Have Not,* I thought his Spanish must have improved a great deal since the last time I had seen him.

Well, that was the last time. But before then, in Madrid, I was able to talk with him about something that was not an everyday subject. The conversation took place in one of those cafes on the "Gran Vía" where, at that time, there were only absurd things to drink: coffee that was not coffee, and so on. Hemingway was carrying in his back pocket a bent-in metal flask, full of something that, thanks to his invitation, I drank for the first time in my life—whiskey. So that afternoon I learned about two things from the Anglo-Saxon world: whiskey and the importance of Mark Twain. Because that was the other item. Hemingway

[1] "¡tiene c . . . la cosa!"—"¡es c . . . la cosa!" (Trans. note.)

told me it was absolutely impossible to understand anything about the United States without knowing Mark
Twain in depth; and he, Hemingway, considered him
the most important writer of his country. Whether he
was putting a certain spirit of paradox (what the
French call *boutade*) into this statement, is something
I do not know, and I do not think it would be pertinent
for me to make any speculations.

At the time (and the hidden shame it caused me that
afternoon was enormous!) I had not even read *Tom
Sawyer*. I had to read this book, which is usually considered reading matter for children, when I was more
than thirty years old. When the war in Spain had
ended and I finally had the time for it, I "plunged" into
Mark Twain. First I read *Tom Sawyer* and *Huckleberry Finn*. The latter work—especially the part about
the liberation of Jim the Negro—made me think of Cervantes. I decided to make a study of Mark Twain's
work some day, to demonstrate the relationship, which
was indisputable to me, between this book and the
Quixote. But the project—as are so many in life—kept
being put off.

After many years, when I came to the United States,
the plan arose once more. I tried to get more information. And it turned out that I had discovered the Medi-
terranean: what I wanted to show had already been
demonstrated long ago. But the study was not wasted
effort for me. In fact, Mark Twain and his work—that
is, the two works I have mentioned—along with Dostoevski's *The Idiot*, are the basis for this study today.

Having stated this, it now seems I must refer to Ortega's quotation which serves as a heading for these
pages. As has happened so many times—if not always

—Ortega has, in my estimation, been courageous in his undertaking, and has hit the nail squarely on the head: in this instance, with the ambiguity of the *Quixote*. He is correct, very correct, indeed. It is a monumental ambiguity. Is Cervantes making fun? And what is he making fun of? I think that when Ortega poses these two questions he is, at the same time, putting them in a philosophical realm. They are reflections that, while stemming from literature, point to some other thing or things: the secret of Spain, what mockery means, and so forth. My aim is much more modest: it deals with speaking in literary terms and *nothing more*. But, of course—and I will also underline this—*nothing less*.

Perhaps it would be best to cite here two or three paragraphs from *Meditations on the Quixote* so that I can make myself better understood. Ortega writes:

Nevertheless, the errors which have arisen from considering *Don Quixote* in isolation are indeed grotesque. Some, with charming foresight, counsel us not to be Quixotes; and others, following the most current views, invite us to an absurd existence, full of extravagant gestures. [P. 17]

And a little later he says:

The case of the *Quixote*, in this as in all respects, is truly representative. Could there be any book more profound than this humble novel with its burlesque air? And yet, what is the *Quixote*? Do we really know what it is trying to suggest to us about life? The brief illuminative writings that have dealt with it come, with momentary and insufficient insight, from foreign spirits: Schelling, Heine, Turgenev. For these men the *Quixote* was a divine curiosity: it was not, as it is for us, the problem of their destiny. [P. 46]

We should notice a basic fact here: neither Mark Twain nor Dostoevski is mentioned among the "foreign

spirits." For the moment, let us consider the significance of that omission before we go further. Let us go
back to what Ortega calls "grotesque errors," and, especially, those that "invite us to an absurd existence, full
of extravagant gestures." I do not know whether or not
we should see an intentional allusion to Miguel de Unamuno in these words. But in any case, I do think that
the *Life of Don Quixote and Sancho,* in spite of the
very admirable qualities it has, is largely responsible
for those "extravagant gestures" so well pointed out by
Ortega. For Unamuno's paradox—an autonomous Don
Quixote, who even rivals Cervantes—could seem to
condone any gesture more or less "extravagant."

But in the time that has passed between those meditations of Ortega and today, some books have been
published about Cervantes in general, and *Don Quixote* in particular, which cannot and should not be passed over in silence. Without attempting to mention any
but the most evident names, we shall say that works
like those of Ortega and Unamuno, Menéndez Pidal,
Américo Castro, Salvador Madariaga, to name a few,
are admired today—and rightly so, of course—by all
who are interested in the work of Cervantes. And, perhaps without attempting to have the global importance
of the above, studies like those of Dámaso Alonso,
Pedro Salinas, José Bergamín, on the one hand, or of
Pérez de Ayala, on the other, have done something
more significant in this area than what Ortega pointed
out in his day.

Therefore we are no longer confronted with that sort
of national poverty that Ortega was referring to when
he said that only a few foreigners had concerned themselves with Cervantes in order to tell us something intelligent. But even so, this does not make the original

ambiguity of the *Quixote* disappear. Is Cervantes making fun? And what is he making fun of?

These questions have been partially answered from the philosophical point of view, and from the viewpoint of literary erudition. But still, if I may be permitted the paradox, I would say that even before Ortega had formulated his questions, there was already an answer to them. An answer, let us say, made from an artistic point of view, which I should like to call an internal point of view. But these answers were not given as such exactly, and they were, as far as I know, proposed only by two foreigners: Dostoevski on the one hand, and Mark Twain on the other.

I have said that these answers were "not given as such," and I want to clarify my words. There can be no doubt that neither Dostoevski nor Mark Twain was setting out to prove anything literarily. They did something much more important: they began with Cervantes and continued in the direction he had pointed out. They did this in two different ways, of course, and not only from two different sensibilities, but from two different worlds. The fact is that *The Idiot* as well as *Tom Sawyer* and *Huckleberry Finn* are not limited to being commentaries on *Don Quixote*, but are real artistic and literary extensions, from within, of Cervantes' world. But because of this (notice this, it is essential) those characters are: a child and an "idiot." The importance of this point cannot be emphasized too strongly.

If my thesis—that is, what I have stated in the preceding paragraph—is correct, it would be a justification for the present work. This study proposes two things then: one, to add something (supposing that I am capable of it) to the existing studies that refer to the influence of Cervantes on Mark Twain and Dostoevski; two, (and this is the important part) to attempt a sort of re-vision, a "new" vision of Don Quixote, looking at him, as I have said, through Mark Twain and Dostoevski. Inasmuch as the characters of both these authors are, in a way, descendants of Don Quixote, like the children of any man they will help us to better understand their father. And they will also help answer Ortega's question: Is Cervantes making fun?

No, of course he is not making fun. In some instances (assuming that my thesis proves correct) what Don Quixote does, like Myshkin, is to take everything seriously; at other times, like Tom Sawyer—or like any child—what Don Quixote is doing is nothing more nor less than playing. Playing: not making fun. And the role that Cervantes takes in all this is that of the author of a character who is too serious, and who, at the same time, plays a game in everything he does.

Which game? What kind of game? Forced to give a final answer, I would try to take on a Calderonian voice to say: of life, the game of life: for all of life is a game —and even the games are games.[2]

___

[2] A reference to one of the best known lines of the drama *La vida es sueño* by Calderón de la Barca: "que toda la vida es sueño, y los sueños sueños son."—For all of life is a dream, and even the dreams are dreams. (Trans. note.)

PART I

1

Madman or Sane?

"Is Cervantes making fun? What is he making fun of?"

Let us begin once more with these questions. But now within a limited sphere. In reality, if we hold to the words of Cervantes himself, everyone knows that *Don Quixote* was written to mock the novels of chivalry. Point number one. Everyone knows just as well that according to Cervantes himself Don Quixote is mad. Point number two. Notice that Cervantes does not make these statements just once or twice, but they are a theme that he turns to repeatedly.

So one could apparently answer Ortega's question with a statement documented by no less than the words from the book's own author. According to them, Cervantes seems to be making fun of two things, at least: the novels of chivalry and Don Quixote. Therefore, we still do not know—at least, let us say that we do not know—whether the book was written seriously or as a joke, whether we should read it literally or not.

And if we wanted a more or less esoteric interpretation, which would it be?

This was the concern which the *Quixote* provoked until some years ago. But on the day when someone first looked at certain words in the *Quixote* itself, the question was answered, at least partially, by the book's own author: Cervantes. In chapter xliv of the Second Part, Cide Hamete Benengeli,

asks that his pains be not undervalued, but that he be commended not for what he writes, but for what he has refrained from writing. [P. 834]

The one who discovered these words was very careful to point out the character of literary economy they imply, and also the type of key which emerges, stylistically speaking, from this Cervantian concept: what is held back is even more important than what is said. In other words, the key to Cervantes' style is this: to suggest, more than to say; to sketch, rather than to paint; not to draw the form of things, but rather the shadow they cast. But on the other hand, if we accept—as I do —this phrase as being the real key to Cervantes' style, that in itself merely underlines rather than explains the original ambiguity—the "original sin" of Cervantes. We should ask ourselves: why does he write this way? But before answering, let us notice some things in the pages of the *Quixote*.

One, for example, is the essential difference, which Cervantes points out so many times, between the style of history and that of fiction: the latter should paint things as they ought to have been (i.e., embellishing them) and not as they really were; history, on the other hand, must paint things not as they should have been but as they really and actually were, without adding or subtracting anything. Cervantes repeats these ideas in several books—one of them being *Don Quixote.*

And it happens that here too we have something ambiguous. Because Cervantes, while expressing the theory of the two theories so clearly, begins to play not only with these words, but with their very tenor at the time of writing *Don Quixote.* To clarify: it is not simply that Cervantes says and affirms repeatedly that he is using the historical method (when he refers to *Don Quixote* as a "history," "true history," etc.), but that, internally, he sets the book up before the reader as a historical work. Of course, we need only read closely to see the purpose of this: he wants to heighten the reality of his story. Sometimes he does this textually ("history," "true history," etc.); at other times he does it indirectly, as when he calls his work a translation (obviously one does not translate something that does not exist, that is fiction); and at still other times he uses what we might call subtle and deceptive stylistic devices. For the moment, I will point out only one of the latter type, which we could well call a typifying example.

This device is used from the first page, and indeed, almost from the very first words. I am thinking of the "historical" data of the last name of the main character —and even of the other characters, for it is repeated later with Sancho Panza—Sancho Zancas.

They say that his surname was Quixada or Quesada (for on this point the authors who have written on this subject differ), but we may reasonably conjecture that his name was Quixana. [P. 57]

Let us examine these words. Why does he keep saying that we cannot be certain of his name? What importance could the name have, especially when he will later be called simply Don Quixote? Why did Cervantes not just openly tell us the name of the character? Because of the historical method. History should tell us things as they really were, as we have seen. That is why the "authors" concerned with this case are in doubt. It is obvious that here, when he suggests to us that there are diverse authors, and especially that there is room for "doubt," the historical reality of the character is increased: if he were fictitious there would be no doubt at all, and he would be given only one name— the one that occurred to the author—and that would be the end of it. Of course. It is quite clear—but, perhaps, too clear. Because the fact is that neither here nor in other similar passages is anything completely clear. Basically we see something that says yes—but that also says no—and all with good humor, a good and superior humor, and therefore somewhat melancholy: Cervantes' smile. I do not think Cervantes is really trying to convince us in absolute terms about the realism of "Quixada," but I do think he likes to use the "historical" style for his fiction. That is, he is showing us the front side of the tapestry, while stating with apparent seriousness that it is the back side, and winking at us all the while.

Now we are coming to the main point of this chapter, and we are dealing with an ambiguity here too: the "madness" of Don Quixote. Cervantes insists time and again on pointing out Don Quixote's insanity. But he, in fact, insists on two other things as well. The first is to show us, as we shall see later, what Don Quixote is

like when he does certain things, and at these times
what Don Quixote does is in complete contradiction
with Cervantes' statement; so, here, Don Quixote is not
insane, or at least not so pathologically. The second
statement Cervantes makes regarding this, and it is repeated no fewer times than the first, is to tell us that
Don Quixote is a mixture of sanity and madness, or a
madman with moments of sanity and, once more, as if
he is smiling the whole time.

Before trying to make a provisional summary of what
I have stated so far, I will refer once more to Ortega
who, in other meditations, talks about the mental capacity of Don Quixote. In his *Meditation on the Escorial,* Ortega says:

> Cervantes composed the critique of pure effort in his Don
> Quixote. Don Quixote, like Don Juan, is a hero of slight
> intelligence: he has simple, tranquil and rhetorical ideas,
> that are almost not ideas but rather paragraphs. . . . But
> Don Quixote was a valiant man. . . . He turns everything
> around him into a pretext for exercising his will. . . . But
> there comes a moment in which grave doubts about the
> significance of his deeds arise within that radiant soul. And
> then Cervantes begins to pile up words of sadness. . . .
> Melancholy wells up in his heart. . . . And above all, listen
> to this anguished confession from the valiant man: "The
> truth is that I do not know what I conquer." [Pp. 589–590]

Although in these lines Ortega may have been thinking more about Spain, and the Spaniards than about
Don Quixote himself, that certainly does not make his
words any less valid. And now let us make that assertion even more emphatic by saying that Don Quixote
definitely speaks in paragraphs. Yes, certainly. But does
he always? No, of course he does not, for Ortega him-

self points out that type of critique of pure effort which sometimes results from the very reflections of Don Quixote: "I do not know what I conquer." That is, the author—Cervantes—was not a hero of slight intelligence. Furthermore, Cervantes knew that a person who plays the part of a fool on the stage must never be one in real life.

And so we see that in this aspect, too, Don Quixote appears to have two different sides: one when he speaks "in paragraphs"—the discourse on arms and letters, the one on the Golden Age, and generally in everything that Cervantes sets forth as intervals of sanity. In these situations, Don Quixote expresses the ideas of his age about morality, customs, and so forth. But there is another Don Quixote: the one who, while being of slight intelligence, makes us see the stars—neither more nor less—while alluding to and at the same time eluding the double meaning of these words: the "stars" of pain and those others that symbolize the infinite or, if you wish, true "celestial music" [1]—insofar as there is something in them which is divine and useless at the same time, or perhaps divinely useless in the character.

If we summarize what we have noted up to this point, we can see that there is always a duality of forces present in nearly every page of *Don Quixote*. It is, moreover, a duality of forces that almost always acts upon us to influence us not only in two different, but in two contradictory senses: poetic style—historical style; what is said—what is kept silent; madness—sanity. And finally, paragraphs—effort. So we see that we have an overabundance of reasons for finding ambiguities in *Don Quixote*.

[1] "música celestial": In Spanish, a conceit indicating that which is divine and useless at the same time. (Trans. note.)

Let us look at one of the contradictory aspects we have pointed out: madness—sanity. Someone with good literary insight thought that this ambivalent Don Quixote, this sane-madman, was, "in basin-helmet terms," a twin brother to Hamlet when the latter defines himself:

I am but mad north-north-west: when the wind is southerly I know a hawk from a handsaw. [*Hamlet*, 2.2]

The spiritual connection between the two characters, if there were one, would be in a specific madness in a certain direction: north-north-west. And at first glance this actually seems to be the version that Cervantes is giving us: Don Quixote reasons logically about everything except in a certain direction on his compass: the north-north-west of his notions about chivalry.

But if we look closely we will see that "sixty-six sheep is not the same as sixty sick sheep," as the saying goes. In fact, in that sentence Hamlet is not asserting his madness as much as he is his sanity—his ability, as we used to say when we were children, "to tell the sheep from the goats": like the king, his stepfather, and the queen, Hamlet's own mother. So his north-north-west madness is not only conscious but, in a way, voluntary. I am but mad north-north-west is almost like saying: I am only mad when I want to be, when it pleases me.

Is this the case with Don Quixote? Not exactly. If we hold to Cervantes' version, Don Quixote is a sane man who loses his grasp on reason only when he alights on the north-north-west of his notions about chivalry— that is, involuntarily; in any case, Don Quixote's insanity apparently does not have a purpose, much less a clear and explicit purpose. In fact, there are many examples (conversations with the curate and the barber, with the goatherd who thinks "Don Quixote must have a couple of rooms in his brain vacant," and others) in which Don Quixote becomes like a madman simply because someone dares doubt his reason. We could say, then, that if there is the same amount of "insanity" (of the type that lies in that north-north-westerly direction) in both characters, it is of a very different sort in each. For while Hamlet thrives on pained sarcasm, in Don Quixote, if we hold only to the apparent—but no more than apparent—testimony of Cervantes, what happens is completely the opposite. And to a certain extent, we cannot say this is not so. But I do believe we can say that it is not this way alone.

In fact, there are times when Don Quixote does foolish things and scarcely any mention or allusion is made to topics of chivalry. For if I am not completely blinded by my theme, we are going to see that Don Quixote has his other moments. In some of them it is simply that Don Quixote is not mad, but pretends to be mad; and there are even other times when Don Quixote, like the most vulgar of men, is sane enough to lie —or to tolerate a lie—semiconsciously at times and at others, undoubtedly, with full consciousness. And we are basing our assertion, of course, on nothing other than Cervantes' text.

Leaving for later chapters some examples that may serve as evidence, for the moment I would like my argument to be accepted as a working hypothesis. In which case we find ourselves with a serious problem. Does he lie? Does Don Quixote lie? Does this man lie who, in a way, is the embodiment of truth itself? Perhaps there may be some more or less Quixotified—or

Unamunoized—reader who would throw back in my
face the very words that Don Quixote said to Juan Haldudo, the rich man of Quintanar and the flogger of Andresillo: "Have you the impudence to lie in my presence, vile serf?"

But to see the solution to this apparent enigma we
need only state it in another way. Must we always—no
matter what the circumstances—say that not to tell the
truth is to lie? Don Quixote, even in those proven cases
when he does not tell the truth, is not necessarily lying.
But, if this is so, what does happen then?

I believe what happens is that Don Quixote occasion-
ally talks by means of magic. Just that. And is there
any magic more "magical" than that of a child? Assuming I have shown my intention with these words, I
would like to tell an anecdote here, by which I came to
understand this (intellectually, I mean) for the first
time, in the Palais Royal of Paris. The little neighbor-
hood children are always running around and playing
there. On one particular day one group was playing
"cops and robbers" with another, and from time to time
there would be an armed battle. The "dead ones," of
course, would stop fighting for a while. But one of the
little fellows, tired of doing nothing for so long, tried to
attack one of his "enemies" who answered him
sharply: "tu ne peux pas, tu es mort." The little fellow
saw the other's logic, and stopped. He was cut short
and completely dejected, but the fact is that he understood: you can't, you're dead. Could anything be more
clear? How can a dead person mix with the living? But
the only difficulty I see in this is that in the real light of
truth, as they say, he was not dead.

So we are confronted with a typical case of "magic":

a thing is true, and at the same time it is a lie. To understand it (in my conscious mind) took me many years; but, of course, as far as knowing it is concerned, I knew it at that age too—that golden age—when every child knows about such things.

Now, if we go from the Palais Royal in Paris to the Mississippi Valley, we will find two cases of "magic" used literarily. Let us note before we go on, that both are cited in various studies about the connection between Cervantes and Mark Twain. The first of these cases, which I will call "simple magic," is a dialogue so true to life that I am sure any child of any country would understand it immediately:

They took their lath swords, dumped their other traps on the ground, struck a fencing attitude, foot to foot, and began a grave, careful combat, "two up and two down." Presently Tom said:
"Now, if you've got the hang, go it lively!"
So they "went it lively," panting and perspiring with the work. By and by Tom shouted:
"Fall! Fall! Why don't you fall?"
"I sha'n't! Why don't you fall yourself? You're getting the worst of it."
"Why, that ain't anything. I can't fall; that ain't the way it is in the book. The book says, 'then with one backhanded stroke he slew poor Guy of Guisborne.' You're to turn around and let me hit you in the back."
There was no getting around the authorities, so Joe turned, received the whack and fell.
"Now," said Joe, getting up, "you got to let me kill you. That's fair."
"Why, I can't do that, it ain't in the book." [P. 70]

The second, which I will call "complex magic" consists of the same magic of course, but has, in addition, mischief—or a kind of mischief. It is in a section of *Huckleberry Finn* where Tom, Huck, and their gang are "robbers," and they attack the little children of a Sunday school, "magically" changed by Tom into "Spaniards" and "Arabs." The author of the book puts in Huck's mouth—a skeptical, realistic Huck—certain arguments that could place poor Tom in what we might well call dialectical straits. But Tom knows how to get out of such straits thanks to the mischief I mentioned before:

But there warn't no Spaniards and A-rabs, and there warn't no camels nor no elephants. It warn't anything but a Sunday-school picnic, and only a primer class at that. We busted it up, and chased the children up the hollow; but we never got anything but some doughnuts and jam, though Ben Rogers got a rag doll, and Joe Harper got a hymn-book and a tract; and then the teacher charged in, and made us drop everything and cut. I didn't see no di'monds, and I told Tom Sawyer so. He said there was loads of them there, anyway; and he said there was A-rabs there, too, and elephants and things. I said, why couldn't we see them, then? He said if I warn't so ignorant, but had read a book called *Don Quixote*, I would know without asking. He said it was all done by enchantment. He said there was hundreds of soldiers there, and elephants and treasure, and so on, but we had enemies which he called magicians, and they had turned the whole thing into an infant Sunday-school, just out of spite. I said, all right; then the thing for us to do was to go for the magicians. Tom Sawyer said I was a numskull. [Pp. 268–269]

That is, you can't, you're dead; only here it is the reverse. To put it another way: when there are no reasons—but there is still the will to play, to make up things—everything that opposes the "magic" is disqual-

ified: "you're dead"—"you're a numskull." And that is
why you do not see the elephants, and all the rest. Now
let us look at one of the scenes from Tom Sawyer's
"grandfather":

Sancho Panza . . . now and then . . . turned his head to
see whether he could perceive the knights and giants his
master named. Seeing none, he said at last:
"Master, I'll commend to the Devil any man, giant, or
knight. . . . At least I do not see them. Perhaps all may be
enchantment like last night's specters."
"Why do you say that? . . . Do you not hear the neigh-
ing of the horses, the blaring of the trumpets, and the rat-
tle of the drums?"
"I hear nothing . . . but the bleating of sheep and
lambs."
"The fear you are in . . . allows you neither to see nor
to hear correctly. . . ." [P. 173]

You are a "numskull"; it is perfectly clear. Now, what
I am concerned with on this point is not to show Mark
Twain's spiritual point of departure, since that has already been demonstrated in a much better way than I
could do it, but to show a sort of return route, going
from the recipient to the donor.

Mark Twain, on this occasion as on others, has not
proceeded analytically; he has not tried to reveal to us
the message that the *Quixote*, as a book, does or does
not contain. Instead he, being a writer, has seen the
road. And so thoroughly that he has made only one
change—in a manner of speaking—in the model, but
an important one: the hero of his novel will be a child.

In order to simply refresh our minds about the story,
since we are not presenting a complete summary, let us
say that the *Adventures of Tom Sawyer* shows us an

American boy, an orphan with a half brother, living with his aunt. Tom is the prototype of the bad school-boy because of an excessive imagination. He lives by and for his books, which turn out to be all the more chivalresque because of the historical disagreement, let us say, between his ordinary American world, and the European reading that he thrives on. His escapades are nearly always born from an insatiable thirst for adven-ture. So his behavior is a continuous attempt to recon-cile his everyday life with a fantastic world of knights from serial novels, historical sketches, and novels of ad-ventures, bandits, and so forth, all mixed together. That is, Twain was perhaps the first to see how much of the world of children there is in Don Quixote. And so we have his "correction" of Cervantes' book: A child, doing childish things is much more consistent than an adult who acts like a child. We will come back to this later.

Stephen Gilman, in his excellent study, holds that Mark Twain "draws near to Cervantes—not by imitat-ing but by inventing." And to prove that point of view (to most of which I fully subscribe), he refers to Ber-nard De Voto, who is the editor of a notebook of Mark Twain, *Boy's Manuscript,* which is supposed to have been the original plan for *Tom Sawyer.* In this note-book, "Cervantes is not mentioned, nor does any inten-tion to imitate exist." So then, owing to the commen-tary that Gilman makes on what De Voto discloses, I discovered something essential for my point of view. Gilman says:

The fact is that references to the *Quixote* or to Cervantes, even in what is obvious imitation, are few and far-between in Twain's work. And in the biography *Young Sam Clem-*

. *ens*, written by Cyril Clemens [Mark Twain's son], Cervantes is given no special importance in the literary terrain of his father. [P. 213]

And in a note that he inserts, Gilman comments:

There are some examples in this strange Quixote-in-reverse, *A Connecticut Yankee in King Arthur's Court*, and it seems impossible for certain lines about the "golden age" not to be direct imitations [of Cervantes]. Other examples are not as abundant. In his book, De Voto says that Twain undertook this oddity because of the low opinion he had of the *Quixote*. He declares that Twain found it "dull and lifeless"; nevertheless, since DeVoto seems interested—as are we—in denying the imitation, and since the basis for his statement is entirely in unpublished materials still in his hands, what he has said may be a distortion of Twain's real feelings, and not a crushingly decisive judgment of the *Quixote*. It is not really necessary to go to such extremes to deny that he was imitating. I am basing my opinion on the sources and on a personal letter which I received from him [De Voto]. [P. 213]

What seems to me essential is the very quotation from Twain's text which De Voto gives, and according to which the American author considered the *Quixote* "dull and lifeless." I do not think there could be a more resounding statement regarding the relationship. In the first place, the phrase is very much like the famous one El Greco made, for example, about Michelangelo: "A good man who did not know how to paint." But on the other hand, in the light of Twain's novels, *Tom Sawyer* and *Huckleberry Finn*, we come to an exact understanding, I would say, of what there was of "dull and lifeless" that Twain saw in the Spanish "grandfather." From a realistic point of view, Don Quixote's behavior (doing childish things) contains an apparent inconsistency. And so we have the correction—which is masterly, from his point of view—that the American author introduces: the characters of his novel will not be men, but boys. What we have been calling "magic" is, of course, much more cogent in children: that two boys are not able to distinguish the boundaries between real life and the reality of a game is, to use Cervantes' words, much more "feasible and plausible." So, in Twain's work we find nearly everything essential of Don Quixote and Sancho but, of course, within a creative process and not one which is slavishly imitative. Or to use the very accurate words of Gilman, it is sometimes a sort of unconscious "return to the model." But because he is this—a creator and not a common imitator—Mark Twain helps us see something essential which mere literary criticism has not seen: the highly childish character of Don Quixote and Sancho.

Now we should ask: having stated this, is everything said? Of course not. Don Quixote is not "dull and lifeless," just as Michelangelo was not a "man who did not know how to paint." In both these peremptory statements I think we must see a type of temporary blindness, brought about by that very "spark" the clash with the model (Michelangelo, Cervantes) causes in the creative "I" (El Greco, Twain)—a spark that blackens out the past in order to better illuminate the future of that same creative "I."

Renouncing what we might call a quantitative evaluation of the relationship of Cervantes to Mark Twain, the fact—sufficiently well proven now—is that both of them give us a pair of characters who are evidently from the same family. But because the American ones were born centuries after the Spanish, and since the

American author was a writer and not a mere copyist, he had to give a new dimension to the prototype.

Incidentally, as far as family likenesses are concerned, I believe it is important to cite something that no one—as far as I know—has noticed before. Nevertheless, it establishes a supplementary proof of the relationship—and I use this word intentionally—not only of Don Quixote to Tom Sawyer, but also to the Russian prince, Myshkin. We know of no immediate family of Don Quixote. In his house there are himself, his niece, and the housekeeper. In terms of family relationships: uncle-niece. In Mark Twain's work, Tom Sawyer has a younger half brother—who "doesn't count"—and his aunt. That is: nephew-aunt.

I do not believe that the relationship in either of these cases is accidental. Don Quixote as an adult man with a wife and daughter, for example, would have had to assume a responsibility that he would not have been able to ignore so easily, unless he were completely mad; furthermore, this hypothetical wife—on behalf of her child and herself—would have looked for a more effective remedy to the "departures" of the knight, perhaps not being content with merely asking the curate for help. In short, a secondary relationship proved more suitable in all aspects to the framework, let us say, of the Manchegan knight. In the same way, Tom Sawyer would not have been able to act with the same liberty with his mother as he does with his aunt. For here, if there were no conflict in family responsibility, there would have been one in moral subordination. And so, a mother would only have appeared a victim of the impudent behavior of the child. But Aunt Polly— the enchanting and somewhat foolish Aunt Polly—is perfect for the liberties that her nephew takes with her. He does obey her—yes, and he loves her—of course, but within certain limits. And they are exactly the same ones that Don Quixote uses to limit his sphere of responsibility and tenderness toward his niece.

In a word: the type of relationship is identical, but the order of authority is inverted, as is necessary for Twain's version in which the character will be a child instead of an adult, for greater realism.

As for Prince Myshkin, even though I will treat it again in another chapter, I will make just one point now: he has no immediate family either. Notice this: in books like these—which explicitly mention *Don Quixote* in their text—the respective protagonists are similar, among other points, in having no family. But is this not, in fact, a "family likeness"? And yet, no one, as far as I know, has mentioned it until now.

Returning now to Mark Twain's characters, seen in this light (but not in this one alone, for we will later see what light an "idiot" casts on him), Don Quixote becomes somewhat clearer to us. Don Quixote is not mad. Don Quixote does not really take the inns for castles. Don Quixote is playing. Just like a child.

But if an important part of the Quixotic world is cleared up by this, it does not resolve all the difficulties and all the ambiguities. If we may say that an adult man, a mature man, who plays and continues to play, is not mad, neither does he seem to be the prototype of sobriety that all our surroundings usually postulate as normal for certain ages. Let us look at this in another light.

2

Enthusiast Virtue

As I already have stated, there is a serious difficulty
in everything I have proposed up to now, and it stems
from the contradiction that my point of view presup-
poses: Don Quixote behaves like a child, but he is not a
child. That is why I referred to the admirable "correction" of Mark Twain.

But perhaps there was someone who noticed this inconsistency even before Twain: Cervantes himself. If
that hypothesis is correct, the apparent Cervantian inconsistency would stem from it: that is, madness asserted repeatedly from the outside, while showing from
within and at nearly every step of the way, the nonex-
istence of such madness. But today we can look this
difficulty squarely in the eye, as they say: Don Quixote,
an adult whom the author terms mad, is simply playing
like a child. And, of course, as I have indicated in the
preceding pages, the key to this enigma lies in Dostoevski.

Incredible as it may seem, not one Spanish book is in existence—to my knowledge—which studies the relationship of Cervantes to Dostoevski. The essays by Bergamín, for example, are simply essays and Bergamín's way of revealing himself. His work is not, nor does it pretend to be, a study of this very important relationship that still awaits an author who will deal with it seriously. I mean that it still awaits a Spanish author who knows Russian (for here I must confess—and regrettably so—that I do not know the language), so that the theme can be treated as it should. As for foreigners, in all of Raymond L. Grismer's bibliography only the study of Wolfango Giusti is mentioned—which is excellent despite its brevity. Other than him, the countries outside of Spain have not done a great deal. Ludmila B. Turkevich in her *Cervantes in Russia*, or Yakov Malkiel, when he reviews the book of this author, does not —in my estimation—add much to what was written by Giusti in his day. More recently, thanks to René Wellek, I came to know Murray Krieger's work. Later I shall refer to all these, but to avoid footnotes as much as possible, I must ask the reader to refer to the bibliography from now on, since in the text I will give only the name of the author commented on each time.

Among the various references that Dostoevski makes to Cervantes, some are direct, and these are in a letter dated January 1, 1868; others are in *A Writer's Diary*, expressing his purpose in writing *The Idiot*. They have already been mentioned: first by Giusti, and then by Turkevich, Krieger, and a few others. Let us see several sentences:

A more profound and a more powerful work than this one (*Don Quixote*) is not to be found. It is the final and the

greatest utterance of the human mind . . . [because] man's
purity, wisdom, simplicity . . . go to waste, go without
benefit to mankind and are even turned to ridicule. . . .
[Turkevich, in *Cervantes Across the Centuries*, p. 355]

And referring more precisely to his purpose for *The Idiot:*

The idea of the novel is to present a positively beautiful
character. . . . There is only one positively beautiful figure
—Christ—and, therefore, the appearance of this immeasurably, infinitely wonderful personality is indeed an unques-
tionable miracle. . . . I will merely mention that of the
beautiful characters in Christian literature, Don Quixote
alone is the most complete. But he is excellent only because
at the same time he is comical. [Turkevich, p. 122]

I cannot emphasize enough the importance of some
of these words, especially the last sentence. But it happens that while these words refer directly to *Don Quixote,* in *The Idiot* the author—with absolute intellectual
honesty—makes some indirect references through the
lips of one of the main characters, Aglaia. And her
words are, in a certain way, even more significant. In
fact, throughout several chapters—and not just in passing—Aglaia refers to the "Poor Knight" (a poem by
Pushkin, which is also related to Don Quixote). And
more explicitly still, when she unconsciously puts a letter from the Prince between the pages of a book that
turns out to be—to Aglaia's surprise (who laughs when
she realizes what she has done)—none other than *Don
Quixote of la Mancha.* And to clinch the argument,
when Aglaia talks about Myshkin later, she even says:
"The poor knight is the same Don Quixote, only serious
and not comic."

But now let us look at Dostoevski's intention when

he set out to write *The Idiot*. My ignorance of Russian again forces me to attack this in a roundabout way, since the phrase I am concerned with has variations in the different translations I have seen. The Spanish says: "*pintar un alma pura*" (paint a pure soul), which is like the French version: "*peindre une âme pure*." Turkevich speaks of "a positively beautiful character." But there are differences even in the English, for Krieger translates: "a truly beautiful soul"; words that, after consulting people who speak Russian, seem to be closer to those of Dostoevski. Whatever the case, and with the margin of error there might be between a "truly beautiful soul" and "a pure soul," we now find ourselves before another interpretation of the Quixotic spirit.

To begin with, we must say that it is, of course, another creative interpretation. And here, since the Prince is an adult and not a child, if we cannot say that he is playing, like Tom Sawyer (or like Don Quixote, if we accept my thesis for the time being), his behavior is so anomalous that all those who know him are content to call him—more or less benevolently or angrily, depending on the person—an "idiot."

Regarding this point, let us see a part of the many things that are said in Dostoevski's text. In the pages where Myshkin tells General Epanchin's wife and daughters about his life in Switzerland, he talks of many things. Among them, when he refers to his relationship with Marie—the girl who is like an "insulted and injured" shepherdess—Myshkin tells us about his relations with the children. Let us examine some passages:

But it was after the funeral [of Marie] that I was most persecuted by the villagers on account of the children. . . .

This persecution brought me nearer to the children than ever. [Pp. 97–98]

About Schneider, his doctor, he says:

Schneider uttered a very strange thought. . . . He told me that he had come to the conclusion that I was a complete child myself, altogether a child; that it was only in face and figure that I was like a grown-up person, but that in development, in soul, in character, and perhaps in intelligence, I was not grown up, and that so I should remain, if I lived to be sixty. [P. 98]

And then, at the end of the chapter, when he makes a "portrait," let us say, of each of Epanchin's daughters, he turns to the mother, Lizaveta Prokofyevna, who in the novel may be the soul nearest that of the Prince, and he says to her:

But from your face, Lizaveta Prokofyevna, . . . I feel positively certain that you are a perfect child in everything, everything, in good and bad alike, in spite of your age. You are not angry with me for saying so? You know what I think of children. And don't think it's from simplicity that I have spoken so openly about your faces. Oh no, not at all! [P. 100]

So the General's wife, "in good and bad alike," will always be "a perfect child." But who is it that is saying this? Did Myshkin not say almost exactly the same when he was talking about himself? Why, in order to come to this conclusion about her, did he feel it was first necessary to say those things about the children, about his relation to them, about himself? And we find all of this corroborated throughout the entire novel, by the Prince's behavior. Perhaps the most characteristic note in his behavior is his seriousness. It is a seriousness that, generally speaking, no one usually has except children: that is why he is so candid; and also that is why he is so sagacious. It is an implacable sagacity, I would add, that this "idiot" sometimes shows in understanding the highly complex motives of those around him.

As a result, here too—as in Don Quixote—the complete description of the character demands a kind of double perspective. From the outside, with the insufficient and hurried vocabulary that circumstances and "society" impose, the character will appear to be an "idiot"—Don Quixote's "madness"; but, from within, we see that we are confronting a "pure soul" or "a truly beautiful soul." And if, to the author's intentional beauty-purity, we add the numerous situations that we will see later—although it may be in passing—such as the Prince's own explanation about Lizaveta Prokofyevna, I do not think I will be taking too many liberties if I say that this—the beauty-purity—is what every child has or has had at some time of beauty and of purity. Let me say it with greater words:

At the same time came the disciples unto Jesus, saying, Who is the greatest in the kingdom of heaven? And Jesus called a little child unto him, and set him in the midst of them, And said, Verily I say unto you, Except ye be converted, and become as little children, ye shall not enter into the kingdom of heaven. Whosoever therefore shall humble himself as this little child, the same is greatest in the kingdom of heaven. And whoso shall receive one such little child in my name receiveth me. [Matt. 18:1-5]

That "except ye be converted, and become as little children" seems to me sufficient to cover the highest reaches of Dostoevski's words—whatever they may be semantically. In Dostoevski's work are children not, in fact, a kind of constant to show the superior world? And those who come closest to them—Alyosha Karamazov or Myshkin—do they not seem to be like those who are nearest the kingdom of God?

So now we see that it is possible to be a "child" at the same time that one is an adult. And we also see now that the "dull and lifeless" writing that Twain thought he saw in *Don Quixote* may have resulted, as I have suggested elsewhere, from the American author's having been dazzled by the spark that flared up in his own spirit as a result of his contact with the *Quixote*— to do the novel with children and not with men—and having been blinded to the point of thinking he saw clumsiness where there is really something greater than greatness: infancy-adulthood. Not the "madness" postulated by Cervantes—which is an insufficient explanation and was sensed as such by Twain—but the "idiocy," which those incapable of humbling themselves until they are like children, see in Myshkin. And notice that part of the Cervantian ambiguity still exists here. The Russian author himself does not say that the Prince is an idiot; it is the other characters in the novel who say so; but Dostoevski does say that Myshkin is a sickly man, and that he has attacks.

Having stated this in general—and I will return to it later—and before starting to comment on the relationship of *The Idiot* to *Don Quixote*, I should like to note some strictly and succinctly literary points that seem to me strange coincidences, at the very least. But before doing so, is it necessary to state that I am not seeking in any way to try to belittle the Russian author? In my opinion, and I want to make this very clear in order to give greater strength to my assertion, the novel has continued to be the one that Cervantes invented until the appearance of Dostoevski, who is the first to add something substantial. For that reason, I believe that there is nothing of servile imitation of Cervantes on Dostoevski's part, but I do believe that there is a sort of spiritual contact between two absolutely extraordinary beings. I would postulate this by saying that a reading of Cervantes might have helped Dostoevski to see more clearly within himself. That is why Dostoevski is not afraid to show, nor does he try to hide, what we could in some way consider his source for *The Idiot*.

And even with this, I believe that there is still more. If, in *The Idiot*, Dostoevski openly states his point of departure, I think that in his other novels (those written after *The Idiot*, and therefore after he had read Cervantes) we can find some touches that may, although perhaps unconsciously, attest to the same origin. If this were not the case, we would have to see an absolutely extraordinary coincidence of events.

As an example, let us look now at a particular case. Every reader of *The Brothers Karamazov* will remember that among the numerous incidents that surround the arrest of Mitya, after "the night of the orgy"—to put it concisely—what we might call an absolutely ridiculous detail is given, but one in which we can recognize something like the round brushstroke of Velázquez, which contributes so decisively to the realism of what we are shown. Mitya knows he is innocent of his father's murder, and yet—at the same time—he knows he is guilty of his intentions and of his own passions, so the attitude he assumes before the authorities is exces-

sively complex. On the one hand he asserts his innocence; but when the solution (which turns out to be the
right one: Smerdyakov) is insinuated to him in a de-
ceitful way, he will not accept it because it is too obvious. And he does all this (and this is the important
point here), unwilling to see that the conversation is
not taking place between equal and equally free men
now. For some represent authority and they are carrying out their duties, while he is no longer completely
his own master because he has to give an account of his
actions. The proceedings start to become clear in a terrible way for him when he begins to receive one order
after another. And now comes the main point. One of
the devices used to make us see the slow degradation
of Mitya is to have the representatives of authority first
search him, and then order him to undress:

"Excuse me," cried Nikolay Parfenovitch . . . noticing
that the right cuff of Mitya's shirt was turned in, and cov-
ered with blood, "excuse me, what's that, blood?"
"Yes," Mitya jerked out.
"That is, what blood . . . and why is the cuff turned in?"
Mitya told him how he had got the sleeve stained with
blood looking after Grigory, and had turned it inside when
he was washing his hands at Perhotin's.
"You must take off your shirt, too, that's very important
as material evidence."
Mitya flushed red and flew into a rage.
"What, am I to stay naked?" he shouted.
"Don't disturb yourself. We will arrange something. And
meanwhile take off your socks."
"You're not joking? Is that really necessary?" Mitya's
eyes flashed.
"We're in no mood for joking," answered Nikolay Par-
fenovitch sternly.
"Well, if I must . . ." muttered Mitya, and sitting down

on the bed he took off his socks. He felt unbearably awkward. All were clothed, while he was naked, and strange to say, when he was undressed he felt somehow guilty in their presence, and was almost ready to believe himself that he was inferior to them, and that now they had a perfect right to despise him.

"When all are undressed, one is somehow not ashamed, but when one's the only one undressed and everybody is looking, it's degrading," he kept repeating to himself, again and again. "It's like a dream, I've sometimes dreamed of being in such degrading positions." It was a misery to him to take off his socks. They were very dirty, and so were his underclothes, and now everyone could see it. And what was worse, he disliked his feet. All his life he had thought both his big toes hideous. He particularly loathed the coarse, flat, crooked nail on the right one, and now they would all see it. Feeling intolerably ashamed made him, at once and intentionally, rougher. He pulled off his shirt, himself.

"Would you like to look anywhere else if you are not ashamed to?" [*Brothers Karamozov*, Pt. III, Bk. IX, Chap. vi]

In principle, the only thing necessary would be the order to undress. Having to undress before someone, by their order, would humiliate any man, and therefore the feeling of wounded dignity or, better yet, the loss of all dignity, would have been resolved, artistically speaking. Nonetheless, Dostoevski does not stop there, but adds the detail—a very small one—which interests us here: the dirty socks and the unsightly feet. Could we say that those details are necessary, indispensable, for the scene? Of course not. If any other novelist had written the scene without that part, we would have thought he had done a magnificent job. But by adding that detail, he definitively and completely crystallized the entire process of inner degradation that goes along with external loss of dignity.

Now let us turn back to Don Quixote. In the battle with the wineskins, when the innkeeper—suspecting what is happening—goes to Don Quixote's room, we are told first that everyone went in with him; in other words, the event is going to take place in public. Notice this. And then the incident is given:

Saying this, he rushed into the room, followed by the others, and they found Don Quixote in the strangest situation in the world. He was in his shirt, which was not long enough in front to cover his thighs and was six inches shorter behind; his legs were long, lanky, hairy, and none too clean. On his head he wore a little greasy red cap that belonged to the landlord. Around his left arm he had wrapped the blanket . . . and in his right hand he held his drawn sword, with which he was slashing about on all sides. [P. 364]

Once again: was it not adequate here to show us Don Quixote in his shirt, with a sword in his hand? Was it not enough? In principle, without thinking about his legs, would anything else have been needed for the literary effectiveness of the scene? What indispensable need is filled when we are shown, as in a film close-up, Don Quixote's legs: "long, lanky . . . and none too clean"? Why did he have to be wearing a red cap which did not even belong to him, and which was "greasy"? Here, too, those details make up the final touch of realism for what the author is trying to accomplish. And this—ultimately—is a situation not too distant from the one Mitya Karamazov finds himself in: the exterior degradation of Don Quixote at one of the very moments when he most needs his dignity, this

being a case of a "heroic" fury or of "enthusiasm" in virtue, to just begin to touch on the theme.

To say that Dostoevski copied or even imitated this
consciously would be ridiculous. To suggest that the
scene could have remained latent in his creative imagination seems to me not only plausible but true. Above
all, because Don Quixote's scene is continued, we
might say, into the Second Part, when the knight retires to his room in the Duke's castle, and "about four-
and-twenty stitches in one of his stockings gave way."

I have cited this example—which is not mentioned
in any of the studies concerning the relationship of Cervantes to Dostoevski—as one more typical case of the
coincidence of procedures. But if we keep in mind Dostoevski's enthusiasm for Cervantes' great work, it may
not be going too far to see here, as in other details, a
true "fount" from whose waters Dostoevski more or less
consciously drank.

But let us move on to the main work: *The Idiot.*
Leaving for a later time any essential relationship between this work and *Don Quixote,* let us dwell now on
another of those details, definitive in the art of the
novel. As we recall, almost at the beginning of the book
the Prince, arriving from a foreign land, goes directly
from the station to General Epanchin's house. Notice
that the Prince has no family at all. The Prince goes to
the General's house without a penny, and with a pack-
age of clothing as his only belongings. Not even a suit-
case: only a sort of bundle. An aristocratic footman receives him. And from the very first moment we have a
situation in which the social incongruity is the most
characteristic feature. The footman asks whom he
should announce, and the Prince gives his name as

"Prince Myshkin." He immediately begins speaking familiarly with the servant, asking his permission to smoke—the permission being denied instantly. While the Prince talks, the servant grows more and more distrustful, since the Prince does not act proud with him, the way a "real" Prince would surely have done—according to the criterion that his status as a servant calls for:

The prince's conversation seemed simple enough, yet its very simplicity only made it more inappropriate in the present case, and the experienced attendant could not but feel that what was perfectly suitable from man to man was utterly unsuitable from a visitor to a manservant. And since servants are far more intelligent than their masters usually suppose, it struck the man that there were two explanations: either the prince was some sort of imposter who had come to beg of the general, or he was simply a little bit soft and had no sense of dignity, for a prince with his wits about him and a sense of his own dignity would not sit in an anteroom and talk to a servant about his affairs. [P. 41]

Is this not identical to Don Quixote's situation with the "women of the town" whom the knight also treats in the very same way, without any sense of his own dignity?

The wenches kept gazing earnestly, endeavoring to catch a glimpse of his face, which its ill-fashioned visor concealed; [like the bundle of clothing "concealed" the Prince's true face from the footman] but when they heard themselves called maidens, a thing so out of the way of their profession, they could not restrain their laughter. [P. 64]

Notice that in both cases the social imbalance is produced by a type of renunciation of the "hierarchy" on

the part of the higher persons, which brings about suspicion or sarcasm from "those below." But contrary to
what we might imagine, the true Christian spirit,
human equalitarianism, triumphs in both cases. The
women of the town, because they are treated like
"maidens," finally become somewhat Quixotified—to
use Unamuno's terminology—and La Tolosa, as well as
La Molinera, stop being—for a moment at least—mere
hussies and become true women who first help the gentleman eat and then, humbly but with dignity, help
dub him a knight. And it so happens that the footman
of Dostoevski finally becomes "myshkinized" too. After
the long discourse that the Prince delivers to him about
the death penalty (like the numerous ones Don Quixote gives: to the "maidens," to the goatherds, and others), the footman who at first denied him permission to
smoke, now:

understood most, if not all, of the speech; that was evident
from the softened expression of his face.
"If you are so desirous of smoking," he observed, "you
might be able to, perhaps, only you would have to make
haste about it." [P. 44]

Let us summarize the two cases. In both there is an
incongruity between the norm and what actually takes
place; there is Christian equalitarianism that makes the
higher characters not see the others as inferior, but as
equals—democratically (or, if I may use a pun, "demireptically").[1] There is a similar incongruity in the topics of conversation: Don Quixote speaks of chivalresque
matters and Myshkin gives lofty speculations about the
death penalty; in both cases, if the inferior listeners do
not really understand all of it, they do understand part.

[1] "al prójimo (o . . . a las prójimas)." (Trans. note.)

Finally there is at least a drop of true Christian re-
demption for the lower characters who, when they are
treated humanely, begin to behave not according to
their customary social rank, but according to their condition as human beings.

Giusti is the first, to my knowledge, who talks at any
length about the adventure of the women of the town
in relation to Dostoevski. (Turkevich only mentions it
as one more case of the expression of a general Christian sentiment.) But even Giusti seems to understand
only the general spiritual content, without stopping to
see how much is identical, in my own opinion, in the
literary procedures. In his study—which I furthermore
find the most perspicacious of those I have been able to
see in a language I understand—he refers to the
above-cited anecdote of the *Quixote* in the following
terms:

In chapter IV, Don Quixote has scarcely been dubbed a
knight by a thieving inn-keeper and two poor prostitutes
whom he raises—and this is especially important—to the
rank of maidens, when he comes upon the wealthy farmer,
Juan Haldudo. [P. 176]

And later he again refers to this episode, but mainly
to note the different reactions of Don Quixote and
Myshkin when they are objects of derision:

One important characteristic: Don Quixote does not admit
at any time that he is an object of derision; we need only
remember his first adventure and the angry phrase directed
at the prostitutes who laugh at his strange words, at the
door of the inn which he thinks is a castle. "Laughter without cause denotes much folly," Don Quixote says solemnly,
evidently offended. As for Prince Myshkin, the "idiot,"

**when he arouses compassion or hilarity, he is not discon-
certed or bothered in the least. [P. 178]**

And after noting Myshkin's reaction when Ganya
hits him ("Oh, how ashamed you will be of what
you've done!"), Giusti ends his commentary about this
point:

Perhaps the Christian and Donquixotic figure of Prince
Myshkin never again appears in such complete contrast to
Don Quixote as it does here. Don Quixote, who is also a
Christian, nevertheless belongs to that Spanish people "who
went with a sword in their right hand and a crucifix in the
left, making people in a far off land confess a creed which
they did not understand" (Unamuno). [P. 178]

As we see, no mention is made of Myshkin's scene
with the footman which we examined previously. It
seems to me that Giusti was blinded by Unamuno's
light; and although he did make a thorough examination, with regard to similarities and differences, of the
general contact of Christian spirit in the two books, he
has overlooked this and other very significant coincidences in the literary form. The very fact that he did
not mention the above conversation in Dostoevski's
book is, I think, characteristic.

But if we look at yet another of those details mentioned, I believe we will find that the spiritual connection between Don Quixote and Myshkin is shown to be
much more than a mere general coincidence, and that
it takes on a special relationship. This time it illustrates
Dostoevski's phrase—which Giusti mentions too—that,
for Dostoevski, *Don Quixote* "is the most beautiful
work in Christian literature because at the same time it
is also ridiculous."

Following the scene we commented on earlier—
which definitively introduces the character Myshkin—
he is received by the General, who immediately thinks
he is dealing with a common petitioner. But during the
course of the interview, with Ganya present, he suddenly perceives that he is dealing with something else.
The General asks Myshkin where he is staying and the
Prince replies, for the moment—nowhere; he asks him
if he has any money, and Myshkin, smiling, answers no;
the General asks if he would like a position, and the
Prince says yes. Finally, and because the Prince himself
has mentioned his illness, the General asks him if he
has had any special training, and if, in any case,

"Would your affliction not prevent your taking for instance, some easy post?"
"Oh, it would certainly not prevent me. And I should be
very glad of a post, for I want to see what I am fit for. I
have been studying for the last four years without a break,
though on his special system [he is referring to Schneider,
his doctor in Switzerland], not quite on the regular plan.
And I managed to read a great deal of Russian too."
"Russian? Then you know the Russian grammar and can
write without mistakes?"
"Oh, yes, perfectly."
"That's good; and your handwriting?"
"My writing is excellent. Perhaps I may call that a talent,
I am quite a calligraphist. Let me write you something as
a specimen." [P. 50]

And the Prince begins to write with excellent letter-
ing, while the other two once more become occupied
with their affairs. Their "affairs" are intimate—too intimate. (They have to do with the abject marriage into
which Ganya, although in love with the General's
daughter, Aglaia, must enter with Nastasya Filip-

povna.) But they continue talking of the women, in Myshkin's presence, as if he were not there—or to be more accurate—as if they were with a child—convinced that he does not understand. As we recall, the fact is that he understands too well, and a little later he "butts in" with a mixture of candor and mischief which earns his being called an "idiot" right to his face for the first time. But that is something else again. For the moment let us look at the phrase he has penned so beautifully.

The humble Abbot Pafnuty has put his hand thereto. [P. 55]

And the Prince insists that it is the very signature of that humble man. A few pages later, General Epanchin, with scarcely veiled words, has left the Prince with his wife and their three daughters, so that they can examine him—or what nearly amounts to that. During this session, Myshkin interjects philosophical themes into the conversation (the implications of the death penalty, a subject that he says he has previously discussed with the footman). Then there comes a moment when he again writes the above-quoted phrase with his magnificent handwriting while the girls smile.

Summarizing these pages, perhaps we could say that Dostoevski was trying to show here the simple complexity—if I may use that expression—of a soul who delves into the gravest conflicts that affect mankind and who, at the same time, is capable of being socially proud of something insignificant. Or to put it in better words, a soul who is significant for his total lack of vanity and social malice—which will turn out to be his greatest "malice."

Well, then, what did Don Quixote know? He knew
many important things, of course: he too had read a
great deal, although not "in a systematic way," and he
had understood his readings in their superessential aspects. But in a position to show his training in some
discipline, when the knight too has to demonstrate his
knowledge before the tribunal of his niece, let us see
what he says:

> "Ah, woe is me!" cried the niece. "My uncle is a poet,
> too! He knows everything, and there's nothing he cannot
> do. . . ."
>
> "I promise you, niece . . . that if these knightly thoughts
> did not monopolize all my faculties, there would be nothing
> I could not do, nor any handicraft I could not acquire, even
> so far as making birdcages and toothpicks." [P. 569]

Here the commentary made previously arises once
more. To say that Dostoevski "has taken" this detail
about the secondary abilities of his character from Cervantes, would be absolutely ridiculous. But to deny
seeing how much is identical in the proceedings (precisely that sort of childish attitude toward the "practical" abilities that, quite significantly, are never mentioned again in either book), is, in my opinion, equally
inadmissible.

These touches, of minor importance, like others that
we will see later of major importance, show a relationship not only deep, but also of a form that, in my opinion, goes beyond what has generally been noted. In a
certain sense—on a small scale—they are among those
that would fit perfectly into the title Murray Krieger
gives to his study on Dostoevski: *The Curse of Saintliness*. But, although Krieger sees a curse in Dostoevski,

he does not seem to notice it in the same way in Cervantes' book, in spite of the fact that Krieger's study is one of the works which openly propose that the origin of *The Idiot* is found at least partially in Cervantes. Let us see his words:

Myshkin's initial championing of Nastasya is clearly presented to us in the framework of Quixotism. Aglaia puts his first note to her in a book which turns out to be *Don Quixote*. [P. 216]

And then Krieger makes an allusion to the poem "The Poor Knight" which Aglaia recites, and which constitutes, as we already know, a clear allusion to Don Quixote. He ends the paragraph by referring once more to Aglaia:

She leaves no doubt that she means the ideal to be a lady, the lady whose initials he [the poor knight] carries. And she terms the poor knight the serious equivalent of Quixote. [P. 217]

In all those chapters in which allusions to the poor knight occur, it was obviously impossible to ignore the *Quixote* since Dostoevski himself inserted the title of Cervantes' book. But is this only a matter of "framework"? One wonders if the critic has read the *Quixote* with the necessary care.

For we have already seen that if the earlier examples do not constitute "proofs" (which, of course, are not meant as such against Dostoevski), they do, in themselves, imply something more than a mere framework of Quixotism. Provisionally, they show a similarity in the proceedings which is extremely noteworthy. Nevertheless, the title of the chapter especially devoted to studying Melville's *Pierre* and *The Idiot:* "The Perils of 'Enthusiast' Virtue," could not be more exact. So accurate have I found this phrase that I have adopted it, as can be seen, as a heading for this very chapter. But does it refer to Dostoevski alone? On my part, I think of it as embracing not only Dostoevski and *The Idiot,* but *Don Quixote* and the two books by Mark Twain, *Tom Sawyer* and *Huckleberry Finn,* which are really the first and second parts of only one book. And I will use the phrase this way because of something that I find very significant: the fact that a title, well conceived to characterize one of these books, can also be used to refer to the others.

Leaving the question there for the moment, let us examine one other case of more or less acknowledged coincidence between the books we are now dealing with, before we get to the main point about the relationship —no longer of the books but of their authors.

One of the theories that arises several times throughout *The Idiot* is that of "double thoughts." As a starting point for my objective, let us take Keller's confession. As we recall, he is one of those typical characters of Dostoevski, capable of the very lowest abominations but who, at the same time, still retains a certain sense of honor. This Keller, "myshkinized" somewhat by his relationship with the Prince, comes to him one day to tell him something, but explaining:

To you, to you alone, and solely to promote my own development. To no one else. I shall die and bear my secret to the coffin! [P. 345]

And immediately afterward he begins his "confession," into which he puts more unworthiness than necessary. Because the Prince interrupts him to ask if he has anything more to add, and as he also asks Keller why he has chosen him—why him in particular—for this confession, Keller, surprised at first, answers:

"In the first place, it is pleasant to watch your simplicity. . . . I know there is a really virtuous person before me, anyway; and secondly . . . secondly . . ."

"Perhaps you wanted to borrow money?" Myshkin prompted very gravely and simply, and even rather shyly.

Keller positively started. . . .

"Well, that's how you knock a fellow out completely! Upon my word, prince, such simplicity, such innocence, as was never seen in the Golden Age—yet all at once you pierce right through a fellow like an arrow with such psychological depth of observation." [P. 346]

And after these words and his allusion to the Golden Age—a point to notice—Keller explains how he had been thinking about that confession the night before, but at the same time he was thinking of asking the Prince for a loan:

"a hellish thought occured to me: 'Why not, when all's said and done, borrow money of him after my confession?' So that I prepared my confession, so to say, as though it were a sort of 'fricassee with tears for sauce,' to pave the way with those tears so that you might be softened and fork out one hundred and fifty roubles. Don't you think that was base?"

"But most likely that's not true; it's simply both things came at once. The two thoughts came together; that often happens. It's constantly so with me . . . it is awfully difficult to struggle against these *double* thoughts; I've tried." [Pp. 346–347]

So then, later on—and this is the important point here—the Prince has one of those very significant double thoughts. But in order to appraise it, and since it is impossible to summarize the entire book, let us observe another phenomenon that I also find of the greatest importance for what we will see later regarding Don Quixote. The phenomenon under consideration is that type of double love that the Prince has for Nastasya Filippovna, on the one hand, to whose defense he goes on a certain occasion like a "poor knight," like a Don Quixote; and on the other hand, his love for Aglaia, the General's daughter, which we should perhaps call a purer love. Notice the amorous ambivalence—within an absolute chastity—of this adult who, while still remaining a "child," is capable of giving a start to a superadult like Keller. And the latter is more or less bedeviled when Myshkin, with complete candor, interrupts the confession—somewhat timidly, but with great insight—to ask him if he would like to borrow some money.

Let us continue with the double thoughts. At a moment that we can truly consider a climactic one in the novel, when the Prince thinks he has seen certain signs of love in Aglaia—which for anyone else would be obvious, since the girl has written him a letter that is beyond any doubt a declaration of love—the author of the story tells us:

If anyone had told him [Myshkin] at that moment that he had fallen in love, that he was passionately in love, he would have rejected the idea with surprise and perhaps with indignation. And if anyone had added that Aglaia's letter was a love-letter, arranging a tryst with a lover, he would have been hotly ashamed. . . . All this was perfectly sincere, and he never once doubted it, or admitted the slightest "double" thought of a possibility of the girl's loving him. [P. 402]

But, really, could we not say the same, almost exactly the same, about Don Quixote's relationship with Altisidora? Or even with the innkeeper's daughter, in the First Part? If the reader troubles to examine the chapter, *The Loves of Don Quixote,* I do not believe there can be the slightest doubt: Don Quixote has his double thoughts too. Regarding this point—and again I refer to the relevant chapter—the Arabic "historian" tells us a great deal; but Cervantes, with his silence—his cunning silence, to be precise—tells us much more. But we might not have seen all this as clearly as we do today without Dostoevski's theory of the double thoughts. For Nietzsche did not write his oft-quoted words in vain: "Dostoevski is the only man who has taught me something about psychology."

Now let us look at the explicit allusions that Dostoevski makes to Cervantes in this book. And to do this, let us see a few of the many lines that talk about the "poor knight." Aglaia, by way of introduction to reading the poem, says:

[the poem] describes a man who is capable of an ideal, and what's more, a man who having once set an ideal before him has faith in it, and having faith in it gives up his life blindly to it. [P. 282]

And then she adds:

It must be admitted that to be capable of such a feeling means a great deal and that such feelings leave behind a profound impression, very, from one point of view, laudable, as with Don Quixote, for instance. The "poor knight" is the same Don Quixote, only serious and not comic. [P. 283]

That is, it is Aglaia—and not Dostoevski in this case —who identifies her hero with Don Quixote, but with this reservation: "only serious and not comic." But the reservation, as we shall see, comes from Aglaia's enamored heart and in a moment of great exaltation. Actually, she knows the truth about the seriousness of her knight. So, in the scene that is preparatory to the final one, to the great reception that—socially speaking—will be the decisive "test," where Myshkin breaks the china vase, and then has an attack; or when the two of them play cards; or at the moment that we have already seen, when Myshkin copies that phrase with magnificent handwriting, she—Aglaia—knows the truth. But, of course, Dostoevski knows it much better since he appreciated the Spanish character for that "ridiculous" aspect, inseparable from and undeniable to his lot as a "poor knight." Let us delve a little more deeply, then, into the question of that amorous duality in Don Quixote and Myshkin.

This is a case now of appreciating the inadequate behavior, let us say, which both of the poor knights show before certain aspects of what, to be brief, I shall call "the eternal woman." That is, the inexhaustible capacity on both their parts for taking women seriously, even when the women do not want such a thing to happen. Now this may be one more insignificant detail by itself, but when added to the others we have pointed out, it does acquire significance.

Much later in the Russian novel, after Aglaia's letter-declaration and after the amorous rendezvous at the garden bench, there occurs the reception-test that I mentioned previously. As a preparation for it, Aglaia has thought it best to give her suitor some practical instructions: he must not talk about serious things, discuss anything heatedly, or touch on such themes as the death penalty, for example; and above all he must not break the famous china vase that the General's wife is so fond of. In a word, he is to behave correctly, "well," urbanely. As it will be remembered, exactly the opposite happens: the Prince gets into a discussion, talks about the death penalty, and finally breaks the vase. There comes a moment when poor Aglaia, with a suitor like hers, does not know what to do; and here one of those unique scenes is inserted that holds the detail important for us. After Aglaia has been gone for a good while, she comes back into the drawing room and tries to dispel the tension that prevails there by inviting Myshkin to play:

[The sisters told the mother that Aglaia had] asked Myshkin to play chess; that the Prince did not know how to play and Aglaia had beaten him at once; that she was very lively and had scolded the Prince, who was horribly ashamed of his ignorance; she had laughed at him dreadfully. . . . Then she suggested a game of cards, *duraki*. But that had turned out quite the other way. The Prince played *duraki* in masterly fashion, like a professor; Aglaia had even cheated and changed cards, and had stolen tricks from under his very nose, and yet he had made a "fool" of her five times running. Aglaia got fearfully angry, quite forgot herself, in fact; she said such biting and horrid things to the Prince that at last he left off laughing and turned quite pale. [Pp. 558–559]

To begin with, notice the implication: in the "intellectual" game she wins and laughs at him; but at *duraki*—which we might translate as the "donkey's game" since literally it means "fool"—he, like a "child," plays masterfully and gives her a terrific "beating." And when she gets angry, he turns pale. In other words, he takes everything she says or does seriously, because he has no malice.

Well then, what happens to Don Quixote with Altisidora? Although I have already referred the reader to the relevant chapter, it seems necessary to give it a certain amount of attention here. Let us look at a few lines:

No sooner did Altisidora see him approaching than she feigned a swooning fit and straightaway sank into the arms of her friend, who hastily began to unfasten her bodice. When Don Quixote saw this, he turned to the damsel, saying: "I now know the meaning of this swooning." [P. 850]

And in another chapter, when Altisidora accuses him of having taken some garters from her:

While the doleful Altisidora was making her complaint, Don Quixote stood gazing at her, and without a word of reply, he turned to Sancho and said: "By the life of your forefathers, Sancho, I conjure you to tell me the truth. Tell me, have you by any chance got the three kerchiefs and the garters this love-sick girl is talking about?" [P. 933]

In both cases are these "attitudes" not contrary to the most elementary sort of Don-Juanism? But, why is this? The answer, I believe, is the same as it was for Myshkin: because everything that Altisidora says and does Don Quixote takes seriously—like a child.

In short (and referring to the two "poor knights" now), they are both pure-beautiful souls on whom feminine mischief does not have the desired effect; and it happens this way precisely because they take the displays of the "eternal woman" at face value.

Finally, we come to the most important point. One of Dostoevski's boldest theses is what we might call a theory of "outrage on the soul." It is formulated for the first time in this book, and even though its center, one might say, is Myshkin, it goes beyond him, not only because of the dimensions it assumes here, but because it is actually an extremely vital question in all of Dostoevski's works.

Here again I am stumbling with the different translations. The Spanish text offers *"afrenta."* A French translation says *"attentat."* And in English we read "outrage"—which seems to be closest to the Russian text. But whether it is *afrenta, attentat,* or outrage, what is clear is Dostoevski's purpose in referring to something that affects the soul. As I say, this theory is expounded in *The Idiot,* but it is really latent in all the works of the Russian writer.

There are some phrases of his that—very significantly, in my estimation—have become well known even out of context. Everyone remembers "if there is no God, everything is permissible." Perhaps not as familiar, although I think it should be as well known or even more so, is Myshkin's sentence when he sums up a concept of Aglaia's: "That is only justice, and so it is unjust." This latter phrase is particularly interesting here because of its evident contact with the theory of "outrage on the soul." With this in mind, let us see how this theory appears in *The Idiot.*

From the first pages, when Myshkin arrives at General Epanchin's house, he engages the footman in a democratic conversation, which quickly strays to transcendental themes. Myshkin says that in France he saw the execution of Legros, who came to the gallows "weeping and as white as paper":

Isn't it incredible? Isn't it awful? Who cries for fear? I'd no idea that a grown man, not a child, a man who never cried, a man of forty-five, could cry for fear! What must be passing in the soul at such a moment; to what anguish it must be brought! It's an outrage on the soul, that's what it is! [P. 43]

The footman to whom Myshkin makes these reflections, and who, we are told, was probably "a man of imagination," suggests that the guillotine may be a good thing because: "at least there is not much pain when the head falls off." Myshkin argues the point, saying that perhaps the guillotine really was invented with that in mind, but he explains his viewpoint according to which the horrible part is not the physical suffering in itself. And here Myshkin, moved by a paroxysm that we could well include in Krieger's "enthusiast virtue," adds:

But the idea occured to me . . . that perhaps it made it worse. . . . Think! if there were torture, for instance, there would be suffering and wounds, bodily agony, and so all that would distract the mind from spiritual suffering, so that one would only be tortured by wounds till one died. But the chief and worst pain may not be in the bodily suffering but in ones knowing for certain that in an hour, and then in ten minutes, and then in half a minute, and then now, at the very moment, the soul will leave the body and that one will cease to be a man and that that's bound to happen; the worst part of it is that it's *certain*. . . . To kill for murder is a punishment incomparably worse than the crime itself. Murder by legal sentence is immeasurably more terrible than murder by brigands. [Pp. 43–44]

Because, with any other kind of death, there is hope, but with the death sentence,

all that last hope, which makes dying ten times as easy, is taken away *for certain*. There is the sentence, and the whole awful torture lies in the fact that there is certainly

no escape, and there is no torture in the world more terrible. You may lead a soldier out and set him facing the
cannon in battle and fire at him and he'll still hope; but
read a sentence of certain death over that same soldier,
and he will go out of his mind or burst into tears. Who can
tell whether human nature is able to bear this without
madness? Why this hideous, useless, unnecessary outrage?
[P. 44]

Later on, Myshkin returns to the theme, not with the
footman this time, but with the General's wife and her
daughters, telling them what a "man condemned to
die" had told him. As we recall, they have led this condemned man to the scaffold and read the death sentence to him right there. And although he has only five
minutes left—which seems like an infinite time to him
—he decides to divide that time: two minutes for taking leave of his comrades; another two for thinking;
and finally one to look about him "for the last time"
—but when that moment arrives, he is incapable of
thinking "either about himself or about anything."

For the moment let us consider this type of exaggerated desire for exactness when the condemned man
tries to systematically divide a space of time that is already ridiculously short—five minutes—so that afterward he can better contemplate no less than the final
collapse of the soul itself. While this particular condemned man knows he is alive, his soul feels alive too,
and as a result his brain still functions in a vital way:
with that desperate perseverance for final order; but
when he feels in his soul—if I may put it this way—the
futility of all order, his brain stops functioning and his
entire being succumbs to a definitive collapse, because
of the injury—or outrage—inflicted on his soul.

But if we move from the psychological to the artistic
plane now, we will notice two things. One, that Dostoevski's originality here is not based on the postulation
that the death penalty as a punishment for the crime is
worse than the crime itself. Up to this point it is a
moral idea and, as Myshkin himself tells the footman,
others had thought of it before him. What I consider
truly original is that theory of outrage on the soul,
which the mere fact of knowing for certain implies for
the condemned man. The second observation consists
of noting that the theory is formulated in precisely this
book in which the reading of *Don Quixote* is explicitly
mentioned. With this in mind, let us return once more
to Aglaia's instructions for the important gathering.
Among them, as we have seen, is the one of not talking
about the death penalty. Let us look at the text:

> "I'll bet anything you'll begin talking on some serious,
> learned, lofty subject. That will be . . . tactful."
> "I think that would be stupid . . . if it's not appropriate."
> "Listen, once for all," said Aglaia, losing all patience. "If
> you talk about anything like capital punishment . . . or of
> how 'beauty will save the world' . . . of course I should be
> delighted and laugh at it . . . but I warn you, never show
> yourself before me again!" [Pp. 575–576]

A wasted effort, as we know, since in an absolutely
Quixotic way—and even comically now (and this is
significant: even comically)—the Prince will end up
doing the opposite of everything the prudent Aglaia
has advised him. I think the most important thing
about all this is that the author thought it necessary to
have the female character mention among the "taboo"
subjects, that one about the death penalty. I believe

this shows that the author knows in his own mind he is still not finished.

And, in fact, he is not. The phrase cited earlier: "That is only justice, and so it is unjust" implies, I think, the whole theory of "outrage on the soul." For this reason, let us dwell on these words. As we see, they tentatively point out a lack: "That is *only* justice . . ." But in reality, what more could justice want than to be just? Here Dostoevski's Christian conscience answers for us: for there really to be justice, there also must be love and charity. To be really humane justice the greatest legal exactitude would never exclude a basis of love. "He that is without sin." In Spain, despite the Catholicism (to show in some way the extreme aversion the Russian author felt toward the Roman Church)—in Spain, I repeat, something like that must have been felt at one time when that phrase so steeped in Christianity was ordered to be placed at the entrance of some of the jails: "Despise the crime and pity the criminal." For even if it is not always practiced—supposing that it has ever been—that does not negate the spirit in which the words were given.

To summarize all this, perhaps we could say that the outrage on the soul is somehow latent in the process of the transformation of justice into law. Or even better: when justice "degenerates" into law. Or, to put it still another way, in the imbalance—which may be inevitable—between the concept of justice seen from the social level, as opposed to the individual conscience.

Now let us turn our eyes back to Don Quixote in the chapter about the galley slaves. I am not, of course, the first to notice the relationship between *Don Quixote* and *The Idiot*. In general terms—but only in general terms—it had already been pointed out by several people and, I believe, by Giusti better than anyone.[2] But —perhaps because of the brevity of his work—I would dare say he did not draw all the conclusions that, to my mind, are required. Let us note, then, out of simple

[2] The moment seems to have arrived for me to refer to criticism previous to this work. So I will try to summarize, as far as possible in one footnote, everything I have been able to find regarding the relationship. Of course I am going to deal less in this note with those works that, seeming to me more important or more central to my theme, are mentioned more explicitly and in greater detail in the text itself, such as the studies of Giusti, Krieger, or Turkevich.

But before doing this, I want to emphasize something that I feel is not irrelevant to the matter: the fact that Giusti or Turkevich, for example, goes much further than I, since each proposes points of contact between Cervantes and Dostoevski not only in *The Idiot* but also in several other books. And yet, in not one of these works do they mention the specific cases I am citing in this text. I believe this apparent paradox can and should be explained by the general nature of their respective works. But it is for precisely that reason these pages are justified: in the fact that excellent studies of a general nature (at times, perhaps, too general) may exist, but have left out or sometimes "blurred," in my estimation, certain aspects that may seem minor when thought of in philosophical or moral terms, etc., but that are important in literary terms. At least, this is the way I understand the apparent anomaly of why books that propose much more than mine, have not examined some of the points I refer to in this text.

In the following summary I refer to everything that has, to my knowledge, been written about the relationship of *Don Quixote* to *The Idiot*—with the exceptions that I make at the end of this note.

I shall begin with Mrs. Turkevich in her excellent book, *Cervantes in Russia*. She—following Giusti, I believe—also postulates the influence of Cervantes on *The Idiot* as well as on several other novels. With regard to *The Idiot*, she states a fact that I was unaware of: that there were seven versions before the final published one: "In the eighth, the hero emerges a totally different type, distinctly Christlike and quixotic, eventually representing a synthesis of three, possibly four, models, all having very much in common—Christ, Don Quixote, Pushkin's Poor Knight and, it has been suggested, Chatski" (p. 121).

But since she herself recognizes the more or less Cervantian origin of Pushkin's poem, the four models are then reduced to three: Christ, Don Quixote, and Chatski. In the final analysis, this last one—which was suggested by A. L. Bem—seems a little forced to Mrs. Turkevich, and she discards it: "Bem's analysis . . . seems, however, to be a *tour de force*. Chatski may have entered into the creation of Myshkin only in so far as he is a representation of an enthusiast out of tune with his surroundings. Spiritually and ideologically, he is really far removed from Myshkin and his other models. Even his attitude to-

propriety, the essential parts of what Giusti says about this:

> We must not on any account forget that between the characters of the "forties" and *The Idiot*, there intervenes the death sentence [Dostoevski's], commuted at the last moment in exchange for the long years at the *katorga*. Dos-

wards women, to which Bem points, has a texture different from Myshkin's. It is passionate, blinding him to actual circumstances, whereas that of Myshkin, Don Quixote, and the Poor Knight is chaste, pure—sexless" (p. 124).

So according to this, as far as sources are concerned, the models would be reduced to two: Christ and Don Quixote. For my part, since Bem's book has not been translated into any language I know, I am using what Mrs. Turkevich has shown as a basis for discarding the model he suggested, as well as Mr. Malkiel's opinion, which he gives in his review of Turkevich's book. Malkiel says: "Bem, in his exhaustive study in 1936, held a brief for the hypothesis [the more or less Cervantian origin of *The Idiot*] (which he complicated by introducing Chatsky into the equation); and Mrs. Turkevich has allotted generous space to the problem (reduced to its original proportions through the elimination of Chatsky) and its successive ramifications" (p. 328).

So, leaving aside Bem's hypothetical addition, let us summarize part of what was said by Mrs. Turkevich herself: "Doubtless Christ was the chief model for Myshkin and Don Quixote the secondary one. The problem of defining the influence of the latter is, however, somewhat difficult because of the resemblance of Don Quixote himself to Christ" (p. 126). And then she adds: "The lives of all three, Christ, Don Quixote and Myshkin, are impelled by a desire to help mankind. . . . The potential of both Don Quixote and Myshkin is tremendous but they both lack the ability to make effective use of their talents. As Myshkin's name suggests, he has the potential of a lion (lev) but the effectiveness of a mouse (myschka)" (pp. 126–127).

She then notes some differences, following Giusti's lead, I believe, and ultimately, Unamuno's: "Myshkin's attitude towards the world—gentle and submissive, derived from Christ—is in direct contrast to Don Quixote's militant one, but there is one aspect of it that draws him away from Christ and unites him to the hidalgo" (p. 127).

But she also points out similarities, although she does it in general terms. In any case, her point of view here is no different from mine, and my only objection is that the statement in her text is a general one and seems to have been written in passing: "Both Myshkin and Don Quixote, in spite of all their abstract wisdom, are infants when confronted with the human factor" (p. 127).

We come to the essential part of Turkevich's analysis when, after noting: "The world refuses to recognize his ideal [Myshkin's], destroys his hopes; therefore, he annihilates the world subjectively" (p.

toevski returns to life profoundly transformed, definitely at odds with occidentalism, and fanatically convinced of the universal mission of the Russian people. [P. 174]

And later:

The reading of *Don Quixote*—and in all probability Turgenev's essay too—have contributed to the transformation of the "weak-hearted" type . . . into the humanly complete

128), she adds: "Dostoyevsky obviously had this parallel in mind. His idealist needed a way of compensating for disillusionment, and Cervantes' device of a psychological derangement was the solution. It is important to recall that of all characteristics given to Myshkin in the first draft, epilepsy was the only one retained in the finished portrait. The reversal of the original concept of the hero and its subsequent development was effected when the figures of Christ and Don Quixote entered actively into Dostoyevsky's creative processes" (p. 128).

Later on she refers to the two characters—but notice that it is in general terms once more—saying: "In *The Idiot* the love motif is just as inseparable from the hero's ideal as it is in the *Quixote*, but it is far more complicated. Two women represent two aspects of Myshkin's *idée fixe*. Aglaya is substituted for Dulcinea, and Nastasya Filipovna for abused humanity, whose lot the champion of Good wishes to alleviate. In the *Quixote* this second aspect is developed in a form musicians call "variations on a theme." Don Quixote defends Andrés, Micomicona, the galley-slaves, Doña Rodríguez's daughter and many others, in various distinct episodes. In *The Idiot* it is developed in symphonic form—consecutive, unified, following a definite pattern with only two figures, Myshkin and Nastasya Filipovna" (p. 128).

After all this, she comes to her conclusions. First there is one about love: "Myshkin loves Nastasya Filipovna and Aglaya fervently, but not passionately. Like Don Quixote, he is ignorant of woman, except as aspects of his ideal" (p. 129). And then, about idealism: "In both novels, the *Quixote* and *The Idiot*, the ideal finally crashes and tragedy ensues. When Don Quixote is deprived of his mania, he sinks into apathy" (p. 129).

Of the many ideas summarized here, let us examine some with which we agree, and some with which we do not. Among the first and most essential ones with which I agree is that of Christ as the ultimate model. As we know, that is what Dostoevski himself thought— he being perhaps the first to observe it with regard to *Don Quixote*. Another observation that Mrs. Turkevich makes is one referring to subjectivization as a final refuge in both characters. And finally—and in my opinion, this is the most original part of her work—she sees the insanity of Don Quixote as a device on Cervantes' part—especially visible, I would add, after seeing Myshkin's epilepsy. On the negative side, I disagree with her on two points: one, the sexless character attributed to Don Quixote and Myshkin. That statement, "Like

figure of Prince Myshkin. Undoubtedly this development in Dostoevski stems chiefly from those internal causes already pointed out; but Cervantes' hero was certainly present in Dostoevski's mind during that important period of transformation. We should recall the previously cited letter from Geneva (Don Quixote is the greatest figure created by

Don Quixote he is ignorant of woman, except as aspects of his ideal," I think is unfounded, and I will attempt to prove it in the chapter: *The Loves of Don Quixote*. I also disagree with the interpretation of the final stages of Don Quixote: "When he is deprived of his mania, he sinks into apathy." In a certain sense—and I will study it in the chapter, *The Moment of Truth*—it is, in my estimation, entirely the opposite.

As far as her analysis on the whole is concerned, it always makes allusions of a general nature. For that reason, the adventure of the galley slaves—for example—is included among several others without being given any special significance.

As for Mr. Malkiel (whom I wish to thank here for the reference he was kind enough to give me about Bem upon my request and because of my ignorance), he does not seem inclined to take into consideration the general influence of Cervantes on Russian literature. In his critical article on Mrs. Turkevich's book, he begins writing with regard to Dostoevski: "who had such a small share of Cervantes' equipoise and serenity, but whose ten years in Siberia, in their effect on his personality and work, vaguely call to mind Cervantes' shorter period of captivity in Africa" (p. 327).

Then he refers to the work of Giusti, who, as we know, held that Dostoevski had created some more or less "Quixotic" characters (Makar, Devushkin, Golyadkin). Malkiel surmises that they were conceived "presumably long before his [Dostoevski's] firsthand acquaintance with Cervantes." But later, referring to *The Author's Diary*, he concedes: "A certain amount of influence on a receptive writer attuned to respond to whimsically assimilated readings is not unlikely in view of this enthusiastic comment on the adventures of the knight errant; but the range of Dostoevsky's experiences and meditations was hardly enriched as a result of an absorbing interest in *Don Quixote*, despite his own encomiastic statement to the contrary. The influence may be defined as the adoption of oddly assorted features of the Spanish novel which, after reflection by the distorting mirror of Russian social critics (indifferent to aesthetic insights), buttressed with exotic illustrations some earlier ideas of Dostoevsky. There is no true affinity; nor did Dostoevsky, who learned a good deal from Balzac and Dickens, owe a heavy debt to Cervantes' literary workmanship" (p. 328).

To this statement, given in a very general tone, as we see, let us add the complete paragraph regarding *The Idiot*: "An issue apart is raised by the much-discussed 'sources' of Prince Myshkin in *The Idiot*. Through express reference to Don Quixote (anent a conversation

Christian literature "because [at the same time] he is also ridiculous."), dated January of the same year that he wrote *The Idiot*. [P. 174]

Here he begins to note some differences:

But it is still necessary to accentuate the differences between The Knight of the Rueful Figure, and Dostoevski's characters which we have examined here: the indomitable

between the personages of the novel about Pushkin's ballad, 'Poor Knight') Dostoevsky made it easy for critics to detect Cervantian overtones in his book" (p. 328).

Some references to other critics follow, among them, Bem—whom we have cited earlier—then Malkiel continues: "Dostoevsky, at the height of his career (when suffering from frail memory), was able to fuse a variety of traits distilled through reading, personal observation, hearsay, and imaginative thinking into an organic whole; it is well nigh impossible (indeed, pedantic) to try to determine the share of each strain even with approximate accuracy. The situation is aggravated by the existence of eight widely discrepant drafts of the novel, showing the transformation of the hero from a sensual into a chaste character. There is no proof that the writer reread *Don Quixote* with engrossing interest during the crucial interval between the sharply divergent seventh and eighth versions. Slowly evaporating recollections of readings in Cervantes, among a host of other thoughts pressing on his mind, were probably operative in suggesting a few extra touches for Prince Myshkin's laboriously repainted portrait" (p. 328).

In summary, as it can be seen, he appears elegantly distant and disdaining, and rather negative—as far as my point of view is concerned. Consequently, and by definition, he has nothing in common with these pages.

Paul Hazard's book would still remain to be considered, one of the first to touch on the theme, and also one of the first to point out the childish character of Don Quixote. But since that book has been in existence for many years and must be known to practically everyone, I will not refer to it in detail. Suffice it to say that, for my point of view, his entire commentary about the relationship of *Don Quixote* and *The Idiot* can fit into one paragraph—and not a very long one, at that; so it too is no more than a general commentary with regard to this point.

Finally there naturally remain outside of my commentary books I have not had direct access to, since they are not translated into any language that I can read. Nevertheless, I will make at least two exceptions for the benefit of a hypothetical "continuer" of my work who may have greater linguistic abilities. One of the books I will refer to is the one by A. L. Bem (see bibliography) because of the "exhaustive" characteristic Malkiel attributes to him, as well as for

battling spirit of Don Quixote has its antithesis, on the other hand, in the characteristic Russian *smirenje* which signifies an entire attitude of non-resistance to evil or supposed evil, of self-humiliation. [P. 175]

He develops this point and then, after referring to the conquest of the realm of faith—quoting Unamuno in his commentary on the adventure of the Toledan merchants—he adds:

Finally the knight enters the arena at other times in order to bodily defend the humble and oppressed against the powerful, the oppressors; in these cases the actions of Don Quixote pose problems of far-reaching consequences, and the first and perhaps main one is the question: Who has the right to impose punishment?, and when and how can such a right be exercised? We shall examine this point in particular because here too we will find some analogies with the Russian, Dostoevskian concept; on the other hand, we will undoubtedly find greater differences than analogies. [P. 175]

After mentioning the episodes of the prostitutes and of Juan Haldudo, the rich man, with the boy Andresillo, Giusti adds:

But much more important and characteristic is the episode of the galley-slaves. Sancho has barely told his master that these are prisoners being forced to go to the King's galleys when Don Quixote explodes: "How! Men forced? Is it possible that the king forces anybody?" All our knight needs is to be convinced that those people are going "by force," and not by their own free will, to feel that the mo-

the many references that Mrs. Turkevich makes to him. The other book is cited in Giusti's study. And since Giusti is still, I believe, the one who has best seen all of this in general, I will defer to his opinion. His author is Prohaska (Giusti does not give the complete name). See the bibliography for him, as well.

ment has come to intervene in defense of trampled justice; for him, the galley slaves become "dearest brethren," and addressing the guards, he invites them, whether they want to or not, to put at liberty "those whom God and nature made free." There is a God who punishes and rewards our deeds. With what right do the guards believe themselves authorized to punish the galley-slaves who have done nothing to them personally? The question immediately arises of whether all this is not very similar to the sympathy the Russian people traditionally have for the condemned man, in whom they see nothing less than a brother, perhaps an unhappy brother. Whatever the case, the problem of crime and punishment is one of the dominant problems in all the works of Dostoevski—the most Russian of the Russian writers. (In this case it is of scant importance that Don Quixote was stoned by the very men he freed, and also that Dostoevski poses the problem of guilt and atonement in all its ramifications, without coming to a practical solution—we might say—to the question.) [P. 176]

This, and what was previously noted about the combative character of Don Quixote, is what Giusti writes about the subject. Then he tries to see the different possible contacts between Cervantes' work and various novels of Dostoevski. But with precise reference to the adventure of the galley slaves, this is all he writes. And let us say immediately that it is not insignificant. But as I see it, he still limits himself to very general terms.

So, for example, if he accurately notes the traditional sympathy of the Russian people toward the condemned man, we must say that he overlooks two things: first—although it may be a very minor point—the real significance of the sign that is usually at the entrance of Spanish jails: "Despise the crime and pity the criminal." This inscription, being where it is, is the greatest testimony to a frame of mind in the Spanish people, which is at least as characteristic as that of the Russian people.

But in addition, and this is his greatest "omission" regarding this point, what is most characteristic about the Spanish people (and here, as he does so many times, Don Quixote becomes a superior type of symbol) is their "enthusiasm" for something we might well call justice on the fringe of the law.

To try to prove it, I will not refer to what happened and is still happening, to a certain extent, with highway robbery. Nor to Luis Candelas. But I will mention one greater example with regard to that justice on the fringe of the law the Spanish people themselves have, in a way, canonized. Fuenteovejuna,[3] all for one, is the sanctioning of insurrectional murder, just in its rationale, although contrary to the law. Pedro Crespo [4] gives arguments to that effect, which in Spain seem so plausible that the very figure of the king himself—incarnate in none less than Phillip II—subscribes to them: it does not matter if you err in small things (and "small things" is the law invoked by Don Lope de Figueroa) as long as you are right in the main thing—having the haughty captain infamously garroted.

But even here we are dealing with secular cases. If we rise to the religious plane, what prototype of reli-

[3] *Fuenteovejuna:* drama by Lope de Vega in which the entire town rises against a tyrannical *Comendador,* and kills him. When asked by the authorities who has done this, they reply "Fuenteovejuna"—the entire town. (Trans. note.)

[4] Pedro Crespo and Lope de Figueroa: characters in a drama by Calderón de la Barca, *El alcalde de Zalamea.* When a captain in the army rapes the daughter of Pedro Crespo, the mayor, he imprisons the captain. Lope de Figueroa, commander-in-chief of the army, demands the man's release. When Phillip II arrives and the situation is explained to him, he says the captain should be punished, but not by Pedro Crespo. Crespo, however, has already had the captain garroted. (Trans. note.)

gious conflict does the Spanish theater consistently propose? Without a doubt, that one incarnate in characters like Tirso's bandit Enrico, who is saved in opposition to the faithless monk;[5] or Eusebio in *Devotion to the Cross*,[6] who also was a bandit for a time. Finally, since the above characters are like his close cousins, we must mention Don Juan, Spanish hero par excellence, and the hero of a highly religious conflict. The perceptive English critic, A. A. Parker, alludes to the "heroic sin" when studying these "types"[7] (if I may play with the double meaning of this word). And to conclude, in this case is not the Don Juan of Zorrilla very significant? Until Zorrilla, Don Juan always went to hell—in spite of the whole world, I might add. But Zorrilla—and this is his touch of genius—"takes him out" of hell and, thanks to the chaste Doña Inés, Don Juan is saved—despite all the serious failings in his conduct. Is it not very significant, I repeat, that today in Spain there is no other Don Juan than *Don Juan Tenorio*—Zorrilla's version? I believe there is nothing that could better demonstrate the phenomenon I call relish for justice on the fringe of the law. And now we shall see, upon close examination of Cervantes' text, to what extent this is true in Don Quixote.

I would say, then, that while Giusti's commentary is without a doubt excellent, it generally follows Unamuno's version—Giusti's principal merit being to have seen the contact that Unamuno's version has with Dostoevski. That is, he underlines in Cervantes' text what there is in it of a radical Christian sense—and so radical! He examines the appelation "dearest brethren,"

[5] Tirso de Molina, *El condenado por desconfiado*. (Trans. note.)

[6] Calderón de la Barca, *Devoción de la cruz*. (Trans. note.)

[7] "tipos": In Spanish the word means both "type" and "an out of the ordinary person." (Trans. note.)

and so forth, which is the general aspect. And in appreciating that both authors—the Spaniard and the Russian—have that in common, he finishes his project. The parentheses included at the end of the quotation is very characteristic with respect to this:

(In this case it is of scant importance that Don Quixote was stoned by the very men he freed, and also that Dostoevski poses the problem of guilt and atonement . . . without coming to a practical solution—we might say—to the question.) [P. 176]

As we shall try to see later, not only is it not of scant importance, but it is of great importance.

For, in my opinion, everything Giusti points out is not enough if we do not look at what is most original in both authors—Dostoevski's theory of outrage on the soul—which has not been mentioned by anyone else to this effect. This is a theory which is also in Cervantes, but which is "written" with that genius of his for saying things by remaining silent. I will try to show this later when we observe what Don Quixote wants the galley slaves to do with their chains: that is, to show us the distance between forced humiliation (outrage on the soul) and voluntary, Christian humility.

It is precisely because all this seems to me a main point in *Don Quixote*—and not only in relation to Dostoevski, but also to Mark Twain—that I have left it for last. So let us look at the adventure of the galley slaves a little more closely. Cervantes, before telling us what Don Quixote will or will not do, is very careful to tell us what the knight sees:

Don Quixote raised his eyes and saw coming, along the road . . . about a dozen men on foot strung together like beads on a great iron chain. The chain was fastened around their necks and they were handcuffed. With them were two men on horseback, and two others followed on foot. The horsemen had firelocks, and those on foot pikes and swords. [P. 209]

That is, they are not only going along guarded, but with chains around their necks, and with all the precautions noted. As soon as Sancho sees them, he realizes what is happening, and he utters his famous phrase: "men forced by the king," which is like a detonator that makes Don Quixote explode and pronounce, in turn, the famous phrase that has been commented on so many times: "Men forced? . . . Is it possible that the king forces anybody?" And when Sancho wants to explain, Don Quixote cuts him short:

Then it is a fact . . . however you put it, that these men are being taken to their destination by force and not by their own free will . . . here is the opportunity for me to carry out my duty: to redress grievances and give help to the poor and the afflicted. [Pp. 209–210]

Sancho replies to this, putting "just justice" in its proper place:

justice, which is the king himself, does no violence to these men, but only punishes those who have committed crime. [P. 210]

And with this, both of them, master and servant, have defined the two positions exactly: social justice or justice based only on law, and justice that is something more than justice: love, charity.

After all this, and filled with compassion, Don Quixote speaks with the prisoners, having asked the guards' permission—even when the historian is very careful to note:

With this leave, which Don Quixote would have taken for himself if they had not given it, he went up to the gang and asked the first man for what sins he found himself in such straits. [P. 210]

Notice first that Don Quixote knows they are going along like this because of some "sins." That is, the meticulous historian makes very sure he also includes a clear perception of the *guilt* of the galley slaves.

Next comes the dialogue with the different prisoners, but I will cite only one of the cases: that old man on the chain who "went along crying" after he was put to shame by being condemned as a pimp "and for fancying himself as a bit of a wizard"—which is the only crime capable of awakening the knight's scruples. This character, seeing Don Quixote's evident charity, breaks his stubborn silence and finishes his explanation with the following words:

But my good intentions could not save me from going to a place from which I have no hope of return, laden as I am with years and so worried with a bladder trouble that does not give me a moment's rest. [P. 213]

And the historian immediately tells us:

He now began to weep as before, and Sancho felt so sorry for him that he drew from his purse a four-real piece and gave it to him as alms. [P. 213]

Now it is not only the knight who has been moved by the prisoners, but human misery—whether guilty or not—has brought out that spontaneous gesture of Sancho, who truly despises the crime and pities the criminal. Finally Don Quixote inspects all the prisoners, and after this the knight expounds what we might well call his own theory of outrage on the soul. Let us look at it:

I have gathered from all you have said, dearest brethren, that although they punish you for your faults, yet the pains you suffer do not please you, and that you go to them with ill will and against your inclination. [P. 215]

Notice this: he calls them "dearest brethren," but he knows full well they are guilty, even though that does not mean they are going to their punishment by "their own inclination." We will come back to this later. Now, after once more alluding to his duty to "succor the needy and help those oppressed by the powerful," Don Quixote adds:

But as it is prudent not to do by evil means what can be done by fair, I wish to entreat these gentlemen, your guardians and the commissary, to be kind enough to loose you and let you go in peace, for there will be plenty of men to serve the king on worthier occasions; it seems to me a harsh thing to make slaves of those whom God and nature made free. What is more, gentlemen of the guard . . . these unfortunate creatures have done nothing against you yourselves. Let each man be answerable for his own sins; there is a God in Heaven who does not fail to punish the wicked nor to reward the good. It is not right that honest men should be executioners of others when they have nothing to do with the case. [P. 216]

Do not all these words really seem to be based on the theory of outrage on the soul? I almost want to say that here Cervantes seems to have imitated Dostoevski. But then Don Quixote adds something that really can and should be referred to by the very accurate expression Krieger uses to head a chapter of his book on *The Idiot:* "The Perils of 'Enthusiast' Virtue." In effect, moved by virtuous "enthusiasm," Don Quixote ends his discourse with the following words—"paragraphs"— which in this instance presage something more than words:

I ask this boon of you in a peaceable and quiet manner, and if you grant it, I shall give you my thanks. If, on the other hand, you will not grant it willingly, then shall this lance and sword of mine, wielded by my invincible arm, force you to do my bidding. [P. 216]

One of the guards shows his surprise and says some-one is going around looking for trouble. "You are a cat, a rat, and a knave," replies Don Quixote, and now filled with his enthusiast virtue:

Without another word he ran at him so fiercely that, not giving him time to defend himself, he struck him to the ground badly wounded by his lance. It was lucky for the knight that this was the one who carried the firelock. The guards were astounded at this unexpected event. [P. 216]

This entire stupendous chapter has already been magnificently analyzed, of course, from different points of view: Unamuno, Américo Castro, Menéndez Pidal, for example, among the Spaniards, and Giusti—as was mentioned. And yet, I feel that some things have still been omitted. The first might be to notice that from the viewpoint of the novel, the adventure here "ends well" —up to a certain point—but, just as Cervantes wished, in a "feasible and plausible" way. And really, given the precautions the guards were taking as they led their prisoners along, it would have seemed all but impossi-ble for Don Quixote to be able to free them. Nevertheless, Cervantes tells it in such a way that there is no philosophical impossibility, let us say, for things to have happened as they did. (Except for one oversight: what became of the guard with the second gun? In the first description, two with guns are mentioned.)

To continue: this chapter could have ended with the freeing of the galley slaves if the *Quixote* were really a "dull and lifeless" book, as Twain thought. But Don Quixote is a pure-beautiful soul. And so, on this occasion, the glory goes to his head because of something that, in its own way, holds implicit the theory of "outrage on the soul." As we recall, after freeing the galley slaves, he tells them to put their chains back on and present themselves to Dulcinea of El Toboso. Could there be a more typical stroke with regard to the "perils" of enthusiast virtue? Could there be anything more ridiculous than this Quixotic proposition? For that, I believe, is the key to the Quixotic spirit.

If Cervantes had stopped with the liberation itself, and if, in addition, the adventure "turned out well"—in this case by being edifying, let us say, it would have seemed to us false, affected, "dull and lifeless." It really needed the touch that by itself, justifies the penetrating observation of Dostoevski: "but (this book) is excellent only because at the same time it is also ridiculous."

In other words, when Don Quixote tells the galley slaves to take up their chains again, this is when he really rises to be Don Quixote. From his point of view, if he was capable of risking his life for the liberty of others, if he brazenly avoids fulfilling nothing less than the King's law for his "dearest brethren," won't they, in spite of their guilt (for who is not guilty of some-

thing?), repay him in the same way? Once freed,
thanks to his efforts, they have then become "magically" changed into free men, and for that same reason,
into dignified men. Telling them to take up their chains
again is, therefore, to give them the opportunity to
show who they are: a thing that actually happens, although not in the sense foreseen by Don Quixote.

For this reason, I believe that in the chapter of the
galley slaves, if we consider the liberation as separate
from the Quixotic proposal that they chain themselves
together again voluntarily, we are deforming something
essential; for it is there the Cervantian concept of outrage on the soul resides. In order to see it better, let us
examine this point in the light of that other novel: *The
Idiot.*

The act of being chained, in itself, is not necessarily
dishonorable nor an affront, nor does it even constitute
an outrage on the soul, provided the chains are worn
voluntarily. When the person is taken by force, against
his own will, that is when the chains debase and offend
or outrage the soul in some way. Let us use the case of
the many penitents who, in their time, used to go about
in chains. In this instance, because the voluntary act is
one of positive humility, far from debasing, it exalts.
But when it is someone else who puts us in chains,
since the act of wearing them is no longer voluntary, it
humiliates and in some way debases or outrages the
soul. The conflict, then, is in the change from punishment to expiation. And just by formulating it in this
way, even the language has now become tinged, we
might say, with Dostoevskianism.

And, in fact, the same distance that exists between
the risk of death for the soldier who fights voluntarily,

and the certainty of death that there is for the man
sentenced to die (even if he is pardoned at the last moment, the way it happened—as everyone knows—to
Dostoevski himself), there is this same distance, I repeat, between the chains signifying deprivation of liberty or not, depending on whether the chains are put
on by force or voluntarily. This is the same, the very
same outrage on the soul, except that in Cervantes it
does not refer to death so much as to deprivation of liberty. That is, the chains become a symbol of humiliation (the negative sense) as well as of humility (the
positive sense). For the change in the word here depends only on will, free will.

In the study that André Gide did on Dostoevski he
tells us an anecdote very pertinent to this case. This anecdote was in a more or less obscure relation to the
chapter on *Devils,* which was prohibited in his own
time and which is generally known today by the name
of *Stavrogin's Confession.* (It deals with the rape of a
little girl who ends her life by committing suicide.) Apparently the Russian author felt a need to "confess,"
not in the usual way, but only before Turgenev, a
writer Dostoevski had not seen for a long while and for
whom he did not exactly have the greatest love. Gide
guesses that he may have chosen Turgenev because he
was precisely the person in front of whom his confession would be most painful. Be that as it may, let us
look at the anecdote itself: Dostoevski goes to the other
writer's house, and accuses himself over and over; Turgenev only listens. Dostoevski repeats:

"Mr. Turgenev, I can find no other way but to say it to
you: I greatly despise myself."
Another wait. Always the silence. Then Dostoevski can
bear it no longer and he furiously adds:

"But I despise you even more. That's all I had to tell you." [P. 107]

And, commenting on the matter, Gide writes:

Humility opens the gates of paradise; humiliation, those of hell. Humility carries a kind of voluntary humiliation; it is freely accepted and practices the truth of the Gospel: "he that humbleth himself shall be exalted." Humiliation, on the contrary, debases, twists, deforms the soul . . . it suffers a kind of moral injury which is very difficult to heal. [P. 107]

And is all this not already in Cervantes' text—partly in what he says and partly in what he holds back? In fact, when Don Quixote sees the galley slaves he does not want to consider anything about them other than the fact that they are "men forced" and "against their will." And in a burst of enthusiast virtue he says that his role as a knight compels him to help those in need. And he does, freeing them from their chains, thus changing them into dignified men when he puts an end to their humiliation. Now they have in their hands the possibility of changing the significance of their chains; for if these were a symbol of oppression before, since the men were wearing them against their will, by putting them on willingly, those same chains would become a trophy of humility. The difficulty is, of course, "justice which is only just"—that is, the Holy Brotherhood (the police force of the time)—would not be far off and, realistically, would try to stop such a change in significance. And so we have the dialogue between Don Quixote and Ginés de Pasamonte with the final result that we know about. At any rate, the transition from humiliation to humility—which could not possibly be more Dostoevskian—is perfectly implicit in Don

Quixote's conduct. Don Quixote never stops being himself, not even when he understands from the beginning that they are guilty, that they have committed sins; nor later, when circumstances make him see the disastrous results of his deed—as the Curate's mischief paints it —he neither reverses himself nor accepts "justice which is only just" because of it.

Let us see the reply that he makes when the Curate —informed of the liberation by Sancho—says that he himself and all his companions have been victims of the freed criminals. And in his malicious attempt to egg the knight on, he states:

Doubtless he [the liberator] must be out of his wits or he must be as great a knave as they, or else some fellow devoid of soul and conscience, for he let loose the wolf among the sheep. . . . He has defrauded justice and rebelled against his King and natural lord, since he went against his just commands. . . . Finally, he has done a deed that may not be a gain to his body and will bring everlasting damnation to his soul. [P. 299]

That is, he completely "hems him in," while poor Don Quixote, worn out by so much accusation in the name of "justice,"

did not dare to say that he had been the liberator of those worthies, but his color changed with every word the curate said. [P. 299]

Let us note here the sort of bad conscience Don Quixote has about the social results of his generous act, so that we can later see what happens to Tom Sawyer and his friend Huck Finn. But for the moment, let us give our attention to Sancho. He, unable to resist the Curate's pressure, says that the liberator was none

other than his master. And when confronted with this
turn-coatedness—let us say—of his squire, Don Quixote
replies with these often quoted and very important
words:

Blockhead! . . . It is not the duty of knights-errant to find
out whether the afflicted, enslaved, and the oppressed
whom they encounter on the roads are in evil plight and
anguish because of their crimes or because of their good
actions. Their concern is simply to relieve them because
they are needy and in distress, having regard to their
sufferings and not to their knaveries. [P. 300]

And if up to here we might be able to classify his
words as a "paragraph," the outburst that comes in the
following words is not a paragraph in any sense; these
words are definitely a "pure effort" or, if you wish,
what Krieger calls *The Curse of Saintliness*:

I came across a number of poor unhappy wretches strung
together like beads on a rosary, and I did for them what
my religion demands of me. As for the rest, I am not concerned. If anyone sees something wrong in what I have
done, excluding the presence of the reverend licentiate and
his holy office, I say that he knows very little of the principles of chivalry and that, furthermore, he lies like a mis-
begotten son of a whore. [P. 300]

It is important to emphasize one thing: in these lines
Don Quixote invokes "what my religion demands of
me" even before his books of chivalry, to justify his action. Having pointed this out, we should say that "justice which is only just" is distasteful to Don Quixote
too. Perhaps because in his pure-beautiful soul there
still has not stopped echoing, "He that is without sin let
him first cast a stone." The fact is that here, as Dostoev-

ski perceived, Don Quixote really appears highly Christian "because he is also ridiculous."

I think that we are now in a better situation to understand the relationship of Cervantes and Dostoevski, at least with respect to this particular point. And I repeat that I am, of course, not trying to suggest any slavish imitation on the part of the Russian. But I do think the contact goes beyond that born from a mere coincidence in the Christian conscience of both authors; that is, of course, the driving force in the two. But there is also something more profound and original in Cervantes' pages Dostoevski not only has seen with his creative genius but has made the rest of us see.

That is, we are not only dealing with something typical and common to the Christian conscience in general, but something more profound and individualized. In fact, only a superior spirit would have been capable of seeing and letting us see the profundity of Cervantes' Christian thought, which is so palpable here "because it is also ridiculous." And to what point Don Quixote is not only (as Aglaia thought—but the author of the book did not) a poor knight here: "comical, but serious." And so serious!

With all the seriousness of a child. Precisely. For if up to this point we have seen the enthusiast virtue contained in that chapter, illuminated through Myshkin, we will see it again through Tom and Huck. But to finish with Dostoevski for the moment, let us say there are many things between him and Cervantes, among them, nearly 300 years. But, nevertheless, the relationship is clear. I could not express it with words any better than those Gilman uses to show the relationship of Cervantes and Twain, when he talks to us about

an unconscious "reversion to the primitive type." That
is, in terms of bioliterary mutation, to the "original
type."

If we return now to Mark Twain's characters, I hope
we will see that there also beats in them, and not in a
circumstantial but an essential way, if not the theory
then the feeling of that outrage on the soul so superbly
formulated by Dostoevski. Because they are children too
—and real ones—and therefore, pure-beautiful souls by
definition. And finally because there is also that ridiculous touch in them that Dostoevski saw as inalienably
united with "the most beautiful work in Christian literature"—*Don Quixote.*

On this highly important point—outrage on the soul
—I would say that the American author is even closer
to Cervantes than is the Russian. And, nevertheless, I
have seen this aspect commented on only in the most
minor way, in the driving-force material. In this sense
we really can consider Olin H. Moore's study as perfect, for he had all the patience necessary to best see
this driving force. And let us say at once what this driving force is: As much for Don Quixote as for his American grandchildren, that act of trying to adjust their
own conduct to a model—taken from their readings,
which are used to govern reality.

If these are books of chivalry in Cervantes' work,
Twain uses magazine serials like *The Count of Monte-
cristo,* historical or "historical" tales, adventure novels,
and others. But having studied the external aspect so
well, perhaps he has not used the same patience or the
same effort to see the spiritual identity there is in all
this. That is, the superiority of spirit which exists in the
three authors and which is naturally carried into their

respective works. But—and this is essential—that superiority of spirit is not directly postulated as such nor is
it in a form that, in order to give it some sort of name, I
will call edifying. Instead it appears in a conflicting
way, inasmuch as the greatest generosity, the pure-
beautiful, is at the same time shown to us as childish
and ridiculous.

To understand this better, let us recall the central
story of *The Adventures of Huckleberry Finn*: it consists of the flight of a Negro slave, Jim, who is escaping
to the free states of the North, helped first by Huck
and later by Tom.

Huck Finn, his mother dead, with an alcoholic and
brutal father, lives abandoned by all, without a family
or home. At the end of *Tom Sawyer*, Huck finds out
about a criminal plot against the widow Douglas and
heroically foils it. In addition, together with his only
friend Tom Sawyer, he has discovered a real treasure
—six thousand dollars apiece. Under those circumstances, the widow Douglas adopts him, and she and
Miss Watson begin to give him an education that, for
Huck, turns out to be painful. Huck's father comes
back to the town, hears that his son is rich and—despite the widow and the judge, a good and honest ad-
ministrator of Huck's wealth—he takes his son to a hut
where he lives with him for some time, tormenting him
with his drunken rages. And when the father goes out,
he leaves Huck locked inside the hut.

One day Huck escapes and, fleeing down the Mississippi, he comes upon the Negro slave, Jim, Miss Watson's "property," on an island. Jim tells him about his
plans to escape to the North and then to ransom his
wife and children, and Huck not only promises not to

tell anyone, but to help him. The other incidents are derived from this plot. A couple of real *pícaros*, given refuge on the raft out of Huck's and Jim's compassion, turn out miserably by selling Jim while Huck is gone. But the Negro ends up in the hands of an uncle and aunt of Tom Sawyer himself, and they keep him in custody, imprisoned in a wooden shed until his owner will reclaim him. This same family is expecting Tom Sawyer to come. And when Huck goes there to find out, on the sly, where Jim is being kept, they take him for Tom Sawyer himself. Tom arrives shortly afterward and—warned in time—passes himself off for his half brother, Sid. After this, Huck and Tom try to free Jim once more—but according to the special "canons" of Tom.

One more point to complete the information: Huck feels a human—fraternal—sympathy for Jim, but on the other hand, among the moral principles he retains from the time he spent with the widow Douglas and Miss Watson, one is not to steal. And it happens Huck knows Jim is Miss Watson's property. Therefore, to help Jim escape is "to steal." With regard to Don Quixote, let us first of all examine a primary difference: the initiative here for the liberation on Huck's part, the American Sancho. Later we will see the similarities.

For Jim—as for the Cervantian galley slaves—being freed is no game: nothing less than his liberty is at stake and, with it, his life. So, we are told:

Jim said it made him all over trembly and feverish to be so close to freedom. [P. 356]

And then, on different occasions we are given the feverish tone that this hope of Jim's, an adult man saved by a child, steadily takes on:

Every time he danced around and says, "Dah's Cairo!" [a
city where Jim thought he would be free] it went through
me like a shot and I thought if it *was* Cairo I reckoned I
would die of miserableness. [P. 357]

[Jim] was saying how the first thing he would do when he
got to a free state he would go to saving up money and
never spend a single cent, and when he got enough he
would buy his wife, which was owned on a farm close to
where Miss Watson lived; and then they would both work
to buy the two children, and if their master wouldn't sell
them, they'd get an Ab'litionist to go and steal them. [P.
357]

But following this, there is something more: the conflict in Huck's conscience:

It was according to the old saying, "Give a nigger an inch
and he'll take an ell." . . . I was sorry to hear Jim say
that, it was such a lowering of him. My conscience got to
stirring me up hotter than ever, until at last I says to it,
"Let up on me—it ain't too late yet—I'll paddle ashore
at the first light and tell." [P. 357]

Now let us see how the liberation seems to the liberator Huck. And here we will observe that for him too, it
is a matter of justice that needs something more. In
other words, from his perspective it is also a matter of
justice that runs contrary to the law. Here Mark Twain
has had the discernment to propose the conflict in concrete and—for an American boy of the times—completely contradictory terms: for if Huck feels the inner
need for Christian brotherhood on the one hand—like
Myshkin, like Don Quixote—on the other hand Huck
has a bad social conscience. Let us look at this in a direct presentation first, when the author tells us what
Huck feels:

I tried to make out to myself that I warn't to blame, because *I* didn't run Jim off from his rightful owner; but it
warn't no use, conscience up and says, every time, "But you
knowed he was running for his freedom, and you could 'a'
paddled ashore and told somebody. . . . What had poor
Miss Watson done to you that you could see her nigger
go off right under your eyes and never say one single word?
What did that poor old woman do to you that you could
treat her so mean? Why, she tried to learn you your book,
she tried to learn you your manners, she tried to be good
to you every way she knowed how. *That's* what she done."
[P. 356]

From that state of mind—which corresponds to
doing something forbidden—we can see the culminat-
ing point of this dilemma when Jim, without meaning
to, in spite of himself, and carried along only by his
own hope, does something that is like rubbing salt into
the wound of Huck's social conscience, when he shows
that effusion of gratitude toward this very Huck ("de
on'y white genlman dat ever kep' his promise to ole
Jim"). But here too, Huck, like Don Quixote, "cuts" the
Gordian knot with one blow: "How! Men forced?"
Here too, a moment arrives when Huck, come what
may, decides for his justice opposed to the law. That is,
he decides for a justice that has something more than
justice: love. Let us see the paragraph:

Jim sings out:
  "We's safe, Huck, we's safe! Jump up and crack yo' heels!
Dat's de good ole Cairo at las', I jis knows it!"
  I says:
  "I'll take the canoe and go and see, Jim. . . ."
  He jumped and got the canoe ready, and put his old
coat in the bottom for me to set on, and give me the pad-
dle; and as I shoved off, he says:

"Pooty soon I'll be a-shout'n' for joy, en I'll say, it's all on accounts o' Huck; I's a free man, en I couldn't ever ben free ef it hadn' ben for Huck; . . . Jim won't ever forgit you, Huck; you's de bes fren' Jim's ever had. . . ."

When I was fifty yards off, Jim says:

"Dah you goes, de ole true Huck; de on'y white genlman dat ever kep' his promise to old Jim."

Well, I just felt sick. But I says, I *got* to do it [turn him in]—I can't get *out* of it. Right then along comes a skiff with two men in it with guns. [Pp. 357–358]

And in that moment, when they ask him who is on the raft—and it is two white men, armed and looking for a runaway Negro, who are asking—Huck, come what may, lies (giving them to understand, ably, that it is his father with smallpox), and he averts the danger; so that by lying, despite his social conscience and the fear he has of the two armed white men, he saves Jim.

But if up to now we have seen the story as an essentially dramatic conflict, and one involving pure souls, it still would not be so Cervantian when reduced to this, I would say, without that other touch of the ridiculous that Dostoevski saw in Cervantes. And in fact, Don Quixote was needed for it—or the equivalent of Don Quixote—that is: Tom Sawyer. When he arrives, everything becomes "clear."

Notice this: *Huckleberry Finn* appears as a novel independent of *Tom Sawyer*. So much so that Huck begins this adventure of Jim's liberation on his own. But there comes a moment in the story when, and in a somewhat forced way too, the character Tom is brought back in. Why? Without him the adventure could have turned out well or badly, and nothing more. With Tom and all his reading of novels of chivalry, the touch seen by Dostoevski is reintroduced—"excellent because it is also ridiculous"—which is what really makes of these two books one lone work, without any doubt.

With this in mind, notice that here too Mark Twain adheres to the Cervantian formula expressed in the Second Part of the *Quixote:* instead of inserting independent stories to avoid the monotony of the narration, Cervantes interpolates new incidents, but does it in such a way that they are a result of the main narrative and are feasible and plausible, which is exactly what Mark Twain does when he reintroduces Tom Sawyer into Huck's novel.

Let us get back to the main point. We were saying that when Tom shows up, everything becomes "clear." That is, with Tom the plan for liberation is carried forward, but in exactly the way Tom knows these things must be done—following all the rules of the law. In other words, in this case, following all the illegal ones. And, in fact, from the moment when Huck decides to confide in Tom about the crucial point—freeing Jim— everything goes along as if it were on wheels—I mean as if on books. But, of course, that first pact was necessary, and since it is, I believe, an absolutely essential point in the American story, I will deal with it at the end, when I am drawing general conclusions. So let us see, first of all, the "style" that Tom Sawyer introduces from the very first moment. Before anything else, the two boys, each by himself, draw up a plan for the escape. Huck reveals his idea:

"Then the first dark night that comes steal the key out of the old man's britches after he goes to bed, and shove off down the river on the raft with Jim, hiding daytimes and running nights, the way me and Jim used to do before. Wouldn't that plan work?"

"*Work?* Why, cert'nly it would work, like rats a'fighting. But it's too blame' simple; there ain't nothing *to* it. What's the good of a plan that ain't no more trouble than that?" [P. 522]

Then come Tom's reproaches to Huck for not knowing how things really happen:

"Oh, shucks, Huck Finn, if I was as ignorant as you I'd keep still—that's what *I'd* do. Who ever heard of a state prisoner escaping by a hickry-bark ladder? Why, it's perfectly ridiculous."

"Well, all right Tom, fix it your own way; but . . . you'll let me borrow a sheet off of the clothes-line." He said that would do. And that gave him another idea, and he says:

"Borrow a shirt, too."

"What do we want of a shirt, Tom?"

"Want it for Jim to keep a journal on."

"Journal your granny—*Jim* can't write."

"S'pose he *can't* write—he can make marks on the shirt, can't he, if we make him a pen out of an old pewter spoon or a piece of an old iron barrel-hoop?"

"Why, Tom, we can pull a feather out of a goose and make him a better one; and quicker, too."

"*Prisoners* don't have geese running around the donjon keep to pull pens out of, you muggins. They *always* make their pens out of the hardest, toughest, troublesomest piece of old brass candlestick . . . and it takes them weeks and weeks and months and months to file it out, too, because they've got to do it by rubbing it on the wall. *They* wouldn't use a goose-quill if they had it. It ain't regular."

"Well, then what'll we make him the ink out of?"

"Many makes it out of iron-rust and tears; but that's the common sort and women; the best authorities uses their own blood. Jim can do that." [Pp. 531–532]

And as if that were not enough, Tom thinks of the obvious necessity for Jim to leave a message somewhere, written indelibly. Let us see one of the messages that he proposes:

Here, homeless and friendless, after thirty-seven years of bitter captivity, perished a noble stranger, natural son of Louis XIV. [P. 553]

But a grave difficulty arises for these messages, since in the shed where Jim is being held prisoner, there are no stone walls to engrave the memorable words on. Tom is ready for that:

I know how to fix it. We got to have a rock for the coat of arms and mournful inscriptions, and we can kill two birds with that same rock. There's a gaudy big grindstone down at the mill, and we'll smouch it, and carve the things on it, and file out the pens and the saw on it, too. [P. 553]

As we see, the proceedings could not be more Cervantian. But on the other hand, as I have said previously, we are not trying to prove here what has already been proven—the obvious relationship of Mark Twain and Cervantes. For me, the main point is to see, through Tom Sawyer and Myshkin, the figure of Don Quixote. That is, what there is in the three characters of pure soul. In fact, as far as this adventure is concerned and in order to see the liberation of the Spanish galley slaves in all its depth, we have yet to see the essential part in the pact made by Tom and his friend Huck. Huck, with the bad conscience that we already know about—rigorously parallel to Don Quixote's—still makes his heroic decision (which we have also seen) to go on with the liberation of Jim, come what may; and when the moment arrives, he decides to inform his idol, Tom, of the whole business. What will he say? Will he approve? And yet—thinks Huck—how could Tom,

none other than Tom, approve of something that he,
Huck, knows is so "bad"? Let us see the boys' own
words. Huck is speaking:

"All right; but wait a minute. There's one more thing—a
thing that *nobody* don't know but me. And that is, there's
a nigger here that I'm a-trying to steal out of slavery, and
his name is *Jim*—old Miss Watson's Jim."
He says:
"What! Why, Jim is . . ."
He stopped and went to studying. I says:
"*I* know what you'll say. You'll say it's dirty, low-down
business, but what if it is? *I'm* low down; and I'm a-going
to steal him, and I want you to keep mum and not let on.
Will you?"
His eye lit up, and he says:
"I'll *help* you steal him!"
Well, I let go all holts then, like I was shot. It was the
most astonishing speech I ever heard—and I'm bound to
say Tom Sawyer fell considerable in my estimation. Only
I couldn't believe it. Tom Sawyer a *nigger-stealer!*
"Oh, shucks!" I says, "you're joking."
"I ain't joking, either." [P. 514]

I believe that in those lines, more than anywhere
else, is what Mark Twain owes to *Don Quixote*—the
book he felt was dull and lifeless. Because, in the first
place, Huck sees the liberation of Jim in its legal aspect
even though the initiative for the act is his own. That
is, he has felt very deep within himself the sense of a
justice based on charity and love; but he is incapable of
defending it in words. So that, just like Sancho (when
he feels sorry for one of the galley slaves and gives him
alms), Huck is on the verge of recovering that true
glory for himself, but cannot lose sight of the legal implications: for Sancho these are the king and the Holy
Brotherhood, while in America, 300 years later, they

become the customs of the times and—if I may be permitted the anachronism—the Ku Klux Klan in full power. But it happens that there is still something more. And in that something more is the touch that I cannot help considering Cervantian: when the good Huck, our generous, honest Huck, so much a brother to Sancho (and also so "insulted and injured" in his class consciousness), with true Christian humility sees that Tom—none other than Tom!—agrees to participate in something so ignoble as freeing a slave, he reaches the point of saying that "Tom falls in his esteem: Tom Sawyer a nigger-stealer!" Here too Mark Twain tells us more, much more, by what he keeps silent than by what he writes. Because now we see fully the conflict that is no longer Quixotic but essentially Cervantian: justice in complete contradiction with the law.

Is there not really, in that "fall of esteem" Huck feels for Tom, the same mark, exactly the same mark we saw imprinted at the end of the galley-slaves episode? Did we not see poor Sancho frightened there, saying that the person who did such a "foolish thing" was his very own master? Has Don Quixote not "fallen" too, at that moment, in Sancho's esteem?

We already know the words that Don Quixote, nonetheless, uses to defend his action: "Was it my duty to know . . .?" Here the knight tells us very explicitly he did it that way because it was exactly what his religion demanded. His religion first, and then his books of chivalry. By this, invoking that inalienable part of his honor—"which is the heritage of the soul—and the soul belongs to God alone," [8] he stands firm and does not retreat even when confronted by the supposed disas-

---

[8] Pedro Crespo's line in Calderón de la Barca's drama, *El alcalde de Zalamea*. (Trans. note.)

ters caused by his act. Tom does no less when poor Huck, incredulous, asks him if he is joking. Tom, with all the solemnity of a serious child, also assumes full responsibility for his acts, stating:

"I ain't joking, either!" [9]

[9] Here we need some clarification.

The end of the book seems to tear down everything that comes before in the novel, when we are told that from the very beginning Tom knew that Jim was a free man. Let us summarize that ending:

In order to make the game more exciting, Tom decides to send "anonymous messages" warning the town. The alarm is effective, and some white men, armed, gather in Aunt Sally's house to block the escape. Then everything begins. In the flight, Tom is wounded by a bullet in his leg. At that, Jim, in agreement with Huck, decides not to go on with the plan rather than to leave Tom without medical attention. That is, Jim actually surrenders, and the white men get ready to hang him. Tom, who had been carried unconscious to Aunt Sally's house, when he finds out what is happening, exclaims:

" 'They hain't no *right* to shut him up! . . . he ain't no slave; he's as free as any cretur that walks this earth! . . . Old Miss Watson died two months ago . . . and she set him free in her will.'

" 'Then what on earth [asks Aunt Sally] did *you* want to set him free for, seeing he was already free?'

" 'Well, that *is* a question, I must say. . . ! Why, I wanted the *adventure* of it' " (p. 586).

An ending which, in my judgment, demands some reflections:

1. The reader does not know this until the chapter that we can consider, novelistically speaking, the end. The last real chapter—barely two or three pages—entitled "Nothing More to Write" is little more than a kind of epilogue which follows the formula: "and they lived happily ever after." Therefore, everything happens in the novel as if Tom did not know the truth. We should ask ourselves: Why did Mark Twain not say before that Tom knew Jim was free?

2. The answer to that question seems obvious: in order to keep the reader's interest. If that had been known before, not only would the interest have disappeared (because there would be no tension if there were no "real" risk), but then Tom's "tricks" might have seemed brutally stupid, like a white profligate, at the expense of an illiterate Negro slave. I think that Mark Twain must have felt it this way, more or less subconsciously, and that is why he holds back this revelation until the end, the ending that is in such contradiction to everything that comes before—in both books—and yet is so consistent with the social and literary points of view. Perhaps a preoccupation with realism played a hand here, too. If, as I propose in my text, the mutation of the Cervantian characters into children (a success from the viewpoint of credulity) is due to this, perhaps that

In view of everything we have previously expressed, I believe we can now see that these are not mere coincidences among the characters of the three authors, but something more. We are dealing, in effect, with a "family" of literary characters who are situated apart from the traditional themes. And I think the fact that they are apart comes from the intent of their respective authors. An intent or purpose that one of them—the Russian—was able to formulate with exemplary penetration (painting pure souls), but is equally present in the other two, even though they may not have shown their intent in such a precise way.

But we do not have to think of that criterion of pure souls as embodying "moral" or "edifying" creatures; they do participate in a superior sentiment, but without falling into a kind of prudish or affected religious painting; they allude to essential problems for the human being, but that does not make them sermonize and reduce that human being to a kind of problematic which if it were one, would postulate some determined solutions from a social catechism.

ending is also due to the same cause; but now it would be negative, for if the resolution that we have satisfies ones credibility—as indeed it does—this occurs only at the expense of the spiritual makeup of the character. With this ending (but only with this ending) the "pure soul" disappears, and instead of being a Don Quixote, Tom almost turns into a "Bachelor Carrasco"—with his badly digested literature.

3. Because of all this, the ending seems to me artificial and contradictory to the best part of the book. So my commentary is made from the point of view of a candid reader who believes in Tom—as if that ending were not there which nullifies everything that came before it.

4. Finally, and essentially: what was important for my purpose was to see how much of the pure soul and Quixotic there is in Tom Sawyer, in order to see Don Quixote better. And even though that ending, in my opinion, destroys the character, I am limiting myself to taking the version about Tom that we have up to the moment when he says he knew Jim was a free man. Because, in my estimation, that ending could not be more anti-Cervantian, more anti-Quixotic than it is, and therefore, in all reality, more "dull and lifeless."

Put to summarizing some aspects that have been noted as in passing, or have not been noted at all, regarding the relationship between these creations, I would say that among them the following should be mentioned:

Neither Don Quixote, Tom Sawyer, nor Myshkin has any immediate family. Tom's half brother does not invalidate this assertion, since he is not linked to Tom by a relationship of authority or responsibility, which, in Don Quixote and Tom, is the essential point. Therefore, with Don Quixote there is the uncle-niece relationship, and with Tom Sawyer, the nephew-aunt relationship. Don Quixote's circumstances being an adult man without any direct family responsibility; Tom's circumstances, a child without a mother to wield any direct authority over him. In Myshkin's case—a lone bachelor— if he has any family, it is vague and far away, so that he too, being an adult and a child at the same time, has no family responsibility, nor is there any authority of this nature over him.

The apparently eccentric behavior demands, in Cervantes, the postulation of a nonexistent "madness," and in Myshkin, a tangible nervous illness to justify, realistically, certain aspects of the character. This point has already been noted by Turkevich, she being—as far as I know—the only one to mention it; although, in my opinion, she does so in passing. As far as Tom is concerned, the "correction" his author makes of the model exempts him from any anomaly, since by his circumstances as a child, his own candid game opens the road to "magic" with nothing further needed. But it is the fact that Tom is a child that, I repeat, enlightens us most about the other two characters and the nature of their "pure-beautiful" souls.

And this aspect—infancy-adulthood—is another of the traits that should be pointed out. It has, of course, already been mentioned—Paul Hazard and Ludmilla Turkevich, among others, allude to it at one time or another, referring to the "infantile nature" of the characters. But in my judgment they do not analyze this aspect in detail which, in the light of Tom, and of Myshkin's relationship to children, lets us see better Don Quixote himself. In the second part of my work I think I have examined this as it should be.

Finally, and I think this is the first time it has been noted, there is the coincidence of what we could call a sentiment for justice on the fringe of the law. In Don Quixote it is shown with particular force in the episode of the galley slaves, while in Myshkin with his theory of outrage on the soul, and in Tom and Huck with the freeing of Jim, moved to this act by a deep human sympathy, an intense love for their fellowman, although still having a thoroughly bad conscience for doing something "forbidden" by society.

If to this we add all the aspects—some general, others particular; some of extraordinary coincidence in the literary proceedings, others noted long before I wrote these pages; and a great many, I believe, not pointed out until now—I definitely think it will help us see *Don Quixote* in a different way from what has been noted in the past about this book by Cervantes.

PART II

3

The First Part of
Don Quixote

Up to this point, I have proposed what we could consider the theory of this work. We still must make that kind of "re-vision" we mentioned, to see if the text confirms our theory. In the very first chapter of *Don Quixote*, after Cervantes tells us:

he stumbled upon the oddest fancy that ever entered a madman's brain . . . that he should become a knight errant. [P. 59]

we are told, a short space later, the story of the helmet:

making a kind of visor out of pasteboard, and when it was fitted to the morion, it looked like an entire helmet. [P. 59]

Then he decided to put it on in order to try it out, and at the first blow he gave it with his sword, it fell completely apart; he put it back together again, reenforcing it with:

a few bars of iron in such a manner that he felt assured of its strength, and without caring to make a second trial, he held it to be a most excellent helmet. [Pp. 59–60]

So from the first chapter there coexist Cervantes' assertion about the insanity of Don Quixote, and the evident demonstration that this insanity does not exist. In actuality, the mark of a crazy man is his inability to be objective in his thinking, or to learn from experience. But then there is Don Quixote's action: he does not want to test the helmet a second time. Why not? Because of the "magic": now "he held it to be good."

But a large part of the childhood magic I mentioned before consists of words. "You can't, you're dead." That is why words have the importance they do for Don Quixote. What does he need to be a knight? A helmet that he "held to be good"; a horse, Rocín-ante (one-time hack); the transformation of his own name, Don Quixote de la Mancha, which is no longer Alonso Quixada: through the use of words.

Is childhood magic any different? Tom and Huck decide to dig a tunnel under the prison shed of Jim, the Negro, in order to help him escape. Tom "knows" that the tools for these situations must be "case knives," and so he rejects the picks and shovels that Huck suggests. Both boys begin digging with the knives. But after a while, worn out, they see that they have not accomplished anything, and they stop and think. Huck asks:

"Well, then, what we going to do, Tom?"
"I'll tell you. It ain't right, and it ain't moral, and I wouldn't like it to get out; but there ain't only just the one way: we got to dig him out with the picks, and *let on* it's case-knives." [P. 537]

Let us go back to Don Quixote. Now the knight is armed. But then—if he is insane—why does he not leave by the main door of his house to look for adventures? The clandestine departure of Don Quixote through the back yard is perfectly clear when "seen" with Tom Sawyer in mind.

Tom is waiting at night for his friend Huck, to go to the cemetery with a dead cat: the two boys "know" that throwing the dead cat in a certain way, in the moonlight and in a cemetery, will definitely cure warts. But even though Tom "knows" all this, he still is not unaware that Aunt Polly is sleeping in a room right next to his own. Incidentally, I have not seen this passage cited in works that deal with the theme. But let us see how Tom leaves his house:

At half past nine, that night, Tom and Sid were sent to bed, as usual. They said their prayers, and Sid was soon asleep. Tom lay awake and waited, in restless impatience. When it seemed to him that it must be nearly daylight, he heard the clock strike ten. . . . By and by, out of the stillness, little, scarcely perceptible noises began to emphasize themselves. . . . And then there came . . . a most melancholy caterwauling. . . . [Tom became] wide awake, and a single minute later he was dressed and out of the window and creeping along the roof of the "ell" on all fours. He "meow'd" with caution once or twice, as he went; then jumped to the roof of the woodshed and thence to the ground. Huckleberry Finn was there, with his dead cat. [Pp. 72–73]

Now I think we can see what Cervantes subtly "omits" here: Don Quixote knows that the housekeeper and his niece (Aunt Polly) are in the house, and so he leaves by the back door (Tom's window) because he "is aware" too.

Finally, Don Quixote is in open country. But as soon as he begins to think, we have, and right from the beginning of the book too, a demonstration of how Don Quixote speaks in paragraphs: "Scarcely had the rubicund Apollo . . . " Does Tom Sawyer act any differently? The "sources," the literature that each draws from, may be different, but the result is the same: in order to do what they do, they have to speak as they do: in paragraphs.

On the eve of the first day, Don Quixote is worn out. He sees an inn that is "magically" changed into a castle, and at the door, the "women of the town," whom he calls "maidens." They laugh, Don Quixote gets angry, and the scene seems to augur a bad end. The innkeeper, just in case, decides to speak civilly: "Sir knight." And at that alone, Don Quixote is calmed: because everything has come true. The innkeeper—for his own reasons, of course—enters the game. That is, "magic" has won out. But there still remains one point, a secondary one if you wish, but not so from my point of view. We are told that later, when the women are serving his meal, "it was a laughable sight" because:

as he had his helmet and his visor up, he could not feed himself, and so one of the ladies performed that service for him. [P. 67]

And it was even more difficult for him to drink. So the women feed him and the innkeeper pours wine into his mouth through a straw:

All this he endured patiently rather than cut the ribbons of his helmet. [P. 67]

because to cut those ribbons would really have been to break the enchantment. And so, like a child—a capri-

cious child—he accepts everything, he bears everything, as long as they do not abandon the game: the
magic.

And now let us go to the arms vigil. Don Quixote has
put his weapons on the water trough. Here again Cervantes asserts the insanity of Don Quixote several
times: "The landlord meanwhile told [everyone] . . . of
the madness of his guest," "They were astonished at
such a strange kind of madness," and so on. But if that
is what we are told, it is not what we are shown. It so
happens that when the muleteer wants to go to the
trough to give his mules water, he throws down Don
Quixote's weapons. Let us stop and think for a moment.
We are told that Don Quixote is insane and that he believes he is a knight; someone opposes him in a very in-
considerate way, and it so happens that Don Quixote is
armed: he has a sword nearby and a lance in his hand.
If he is mad, it would seem logical within his insanity,
that from the rage the muleteer provokes in him, Don
Quixote would have taken up his lance to kill him. Is
that what he does?

[Don Quixote] let slip his buckler, and raising the lance
in both hands, he gave the carrier such a hefty blow on the
pate that he felled him to the ground in so grevious a
plight. . . . This done, he put back his arms and began to
pace to and fro as peacefully as before. [P. 71]

But then another muleteer arrives, and Don Quixote,
intending to do to him just what he had done to the
first one:

not saying a word or imploring assistance from a soul, once
more dropped his buckler, lifted up his lance, and without
breaking it to pieces, opened the second muleteer's head
in four places. [P. 71]

Being provoked into a rage not once, but two times, still Don Quixote does not do what we would think a mad man would have done in his place: spear the insolent men in a demented attack. No. Not only does he not do that, but he restrains himself to giving each of the muleteers a beating. In what book of chivalry could Don Quixote have read about such "democratic" conduct? And since there is no precedent in this case, we must conclude that Don Quixote is acting on his own judgment. And that judgment is certainly not to kill—which would have been excessive—but to give a well-placed cudgeling. And then "repose," "quiet," "tranquility." Furthermore, a short time later Don Quixote lets the injured men go away—provided that they leave him alone: because he is aware.

He is aware and is triumphant—in spite of the stoning—since, half in mockery and half in earnest, the innkeeper and the women dub him a knight. And so, "magically," it has all become true, because everyone has joined in the game: Don Quixote is a knight. But—and this is essential—the knights in his books go through life killing: giants, monsters, and so on, and so forth. Don Quixote, on the other hand, does not kill, nor does he ever intend to kill, not even when the opportunity is—to use the phrase—in his hands. Throughout the book we are told that he gives some thrashings: to the muleteers here; once in a while to Sancho. But several times he has "enemies" at his mercy: Juan Haldudo, the rich man, the Bizcayne, the Knight of the Mirrors, and it never occurs to him that he could really kill them. In this respect, the words to Juan Haldudo are significant: "I am about to pierce you with this lance. . . ." But he does not do it. Why do we have all this? Because Don Quixote, a pure-beautiful soul, "plays" at being a knight moved by the good qualities of knights: defending the weak, protecting the defenseless, freeing those held captive. But when the game is at the point of going too far, Don Quixote knows when to stop. Why does this madman forget then—and only then—about his books?

Let us take a look at him after one of these adventures: after that one with Juan Haldudo. Don Quixote has just righted a wrong exactly as the canons proscribe. And so the knight was feeling proud as he went along, "for he believed that he had begun his feats of arms in a most successful and dignified manner." Everything has turned out so well (it has really turned out "badly," although he does not know it) that his heart is bursting with "enthusiasm." And at the first opportunity—with the traders of Toledo—he wants his "enemies" to confess that "there is not, nor has there ever been in all the world a fairer damsel than Dulcinea of El Toboso." We already know how the adventure ends, and so only one detail of it is important here. The knight falls from his horse, he is beaten with his broken lance, but when he sees his enemies going away, he exclaims in his enthusiasm:

Flee not, cowardly rabble! Wait, slavish herd! It is not my fault, but the fault of my horse, that I am stretched here. [P. 79]

Before, when he was victorious, he actually forgot about his books, being satisfied to use words; but now —when there is no danger for the others—now, his enthusiasm does not diminish. Up to this point, where is the madman? But after this, if we are not looking at a

madman, we certainly are looking at something else:
"It is not my fault, but the fault of my horse." What is
the childish phrase that is used for times like this?
"Somebody else did it!" [1]

In the village Don Quixote convinces a neighbor of
his to become his squire, and when they decide to go
out in search of adventures, Cervantes writes:

**Don Quixote without saying farewell to his housekeeper
and niece, Panza to his wife and children, set out one night
from the village without being seen. [P. 96]**

Why this secretiveness once again? That Don Quixote should want to hide his motives—disinterested and
therefore, we might say, hardly interesting to the housekeeper and the niece—is still understandable. But
what about Sancho? Apparently he is going to make
some deals: to become nothing less than governor of an
island. Why does he hide and leave not only at night,
but without saying good-bye to his wife or his children?

Sancho himself will give us the answer. Speaking
with Don Quixote about the promises he had made,
Sancho logically comes to the conclusion that if he
were a king, his wife would be the queen and his children would be princes. "Who doubts it?" answers Don
Quixote from the heights of his enthusiasm:

**"I doubt it," replied Sancho Panza, "for . . . even if God
were to rain kingdoms down upon earth, none would sit
well on the head of Mari Gutiérrez. Believe me, sir, she's
not worth two farthings as a queen; countess would suit
her better, and even then, God help her." [P. 97]**

---

[1] "Ha sido por culpa del gato!" (Trans. note.)

That is, Sancho, with his "pessimism" here, is actually supporting his master's optimism: he will not accept becoming a king, but he will accept the rank of a count. But if Sancho is so realistic, why does he not tell his wife about his plans? In my opinion it is for one reason alone—but a considerable one: the silence of children about their "affairs," when with adults.

The adventure of the windmills may be the one that has stood as a prototype of Quixotic-insanity. In any case, we cannot deny that here we are at an extreme. Never, before or after this, does Don Quixote do anything similar, having no footing in reality. I must confess that for this reason it is the chapter that provides the most difficulty for my point of view. Nonetheless, if we go on by what I will pompously call a method of compensations, we may see what I want to propose even in this chapter—or, perhaps, especially in this chapter.

In the first two departures we have seen Don Quixote avoiding the people who by definition "don't fit into the game." Well then, does this pure deed not correspond perfectly to that fear we might call realistic? There will never be giants more gigantic than the windmills—and Don Quixote attacks them. Might this not be like any child's game where one can get killed and sometimes does?

Here I would like to make a reminiscence from my own childhood. One of my fellow students in the Colegio de los Frailes in the Monastery of El Escorial—Ramón de Lucas, I still have not forgotten his name—was punished, together with another student, by being made to stay behind and pray in the school chapel until I do not know what hour of the night. But

Ramón, instead of praying, made a bet with his friend as to whether or not he could climb the lightning rod of the steeple and leave a handkerchief tied to the weather vane as proof that he had done it. On the following morning, the handkerchief was waving—and when I say "waving," I'm using poetic license—from the arrow on the monastery's weather vane. So seen in this light, as a pure risk, the adventure of the windmills, far from contradicting the general Quixotic theory, would support it.

Since the battle with the Bizcayne is realistic, it is scarcely necessary to comment on it. Here Don Quixote finds another real cavalier—and because of this, his game gets mixed up with reality without the knight having to do anything further. But let us note the enthusiasm all this brings out in Sancho, who, falling to his knees before his master, asks him for the governship of the island. What will the knight answer?

Take heed, brother Sancho, that this adventure and others of this kind are not adventures of islands but crossroads, in which nothing is gained but a broken head or the loss of an ear. Have patience . . . [P. 111]

A realistic answer if there ever was one. But then, speaking in paragraphs, he alludes to the balsam of Fierabrás, telling his squire that whenever he sees him cut in two, to put the two halves—"nicely"—together and then give him a sip of the balsam, and he'll become "as sound as an apple." Sancho, seeing the business end of it, asks him for the formula of the precious drink. Again, what is Don Quixote's answer here?

Hush, friend . . . I intend to teach you greater secrets than this and bestow greater benefits upon you also. For the

present let me set about dressing my own wounds, for this
ear of mine pains me more than I would wish. [P. 113]

So the "balsam," like the "island," is for a later time
—and meanwhile, since his ear is in fact hurting him,
Don Quixote lets himself be cured by more modest
means: lint and ointment, but all the while he never
stops speaking of adventures—future or past—which
will obscure the present reality. And since, because of
all this, Sancho again heedlessly enters the game too
deeply ("God's will be done—and may the time come
for winning that island which is costing me so dear"),
Don Quixote, on his part, holds back once more—and
at the same time shows us the profound truth of his
thinking:

I have already told you, Sancho, not to worry on that score,
for even if there is no island, there is always the kingdom
of Denmark or of Sobradisa which will fit you like a ring
on the finger, and you ought to be all the more pleased,
as they are both on terra firma. But let us leave this to its
proper time. [P. 115]

Could there be any more accurate statement about
what is happening? Here we have Denmark (real), or
Sobradisa (a "magic" kingdom). "But let us leave this
to its proper time."

Don Quixote and Sancho arrive at the inn—a "castle." And here Sancho's unexpected attitude constitutes, for me, one of the essential points for the thesis I
am making. The innkeeper asks Sancho what has happened to Don Quixote. And Sancho lies—which would
not be so strange for him. But the type of lie is strange
in this case:

Sancho answered [the innkeeper] that it was nothing, only that [Don Quixote] had fallen from a rock and had bruised his ribs somewhat. [P. 153]

Why does Sancho lie? And in what does his lie consist? In embarrassment, of course, in simple and loyal embarrassment for his master; but also in childish complicity when with "adults." If he had had to tell the truth, he would have found himself compelled to tell a whole series of things that he knows very well are the sorts of things "you don't say" in front of adults. When would a poor child, for example, tell his mother that he had ripped his pants while playing at bullfighting! And as though we still needed proof for what I am saying, there is Don Quixote's silence. Why is he mute before that "version"? He is aware, of course.

Of the many things that happen in this inn, there is one that is especially interesting when we look at it from the perspective of Tom Sawyer. I am referring to the balsam of Fierabrás. The time for making it has arrived. Now we must see it being manufactured:

Don Quixote took the ingredients, mixed them all together into a compound, and then boiled them a good while. . . . He then asked for a vial to hold the mixture, but as there was not one in the inn, he resolved to put it into a tin cruse. . . . He, furthermore, recited over the cruse more than eighty paternosters and as many Ave Marias, salves, and credos, accompanying every word with a cross by way of blessing. [P. 163]

What significance should we give to that manner of praying paternosters and Ave Marias which the Christian—the very Christian!—Don Quixote performs? What sort of thing is this of making crosses in order to cook up a "healthful balsam"? Does all this not have a suspicious ring of magic and witchcraft to it? Of course —there is nothing Christian about it, and least of all Catholic. And how is it possible that Don Quixote, so respectful toward the Church hierarchy, appears to us here not praying—at least, what we usually call praying—but doing something that, if anything, is like a ritual of magic. Magic, indeed; but now we are using the word in a very different sense: the supermagic that children play at. Don Quixote, literally and undeniably, is pretending he is a magician who is mixing up a "healthful balsam."

But we are not finished with it yet. As soon as the potion was made, the knight wanted to test it, and he drank all that was in the pot. "No sooner had he drunk the potion than he began to vomit." He went to bed, and a short time afterward, as if by sorcery, he woke up "very much relieved," and attributed this to the beneficial action of the balsam.

Sancho Panza, likewise, considered his master's cure a miracle and begged him for leave to swallow what remained in the pot, which was no small quantity. Don Quixote consented; so he took the pot in both hands, and with good faith and better will, he tossed down very little less than his master had done. [P. 164]

Although this time the results are not so miraculous, for we will remember the foul-smelling effects that the balsam had on Sancho, "because he had not been dubbed a knight." Let us leave the Manchegan knight for a moment in order to see what is happening on an island in the Mississippi. At Tom's instigation, he and Joe Harper have slipped away from their homes to become "pirates." With them goes Huck Finn, the vagabond who has not run away from any home because he does not have one. The three have arrived at the island, and they begin their activities as knights—I mean as pirates.

Tom said he wanted to learn to smoke, now. Joe caught at the idea and said he would like to try, too. So Huck made pipes and filled them. [P. 121]

And they begin to smoke with "enthusiasm." At a certain time Tom states: "If I'd'a' knowed *this* was all, I'd'a' learnt long ago." But the author of the story tells us what really happens:

So the talk ran on. But presently it began to flag a trifle, and grow disjointed. The silences widened; the expectoration marvelously increased. Every pore inside the boys' cheeks became a spouting fountain; they could scarcely bail out the cellars under their tongues fast enough to prevent an inundation; little overflowings down their throats occurred in spite of all they could do, and sudden retchings followed every time. Both boys were looking very pale and miserable, now. Joe's pipe dropped from his nerveless fingers. Tom's followed. . . . Joe said feebly:

"I've lost my knife. I reckon I better go and find it."

Tom said, with quivering lips and halting utterance:

"I'll help you. You go over that way and I'll hunt around by the spring. No, you needn't come, Huck—we can find it." [P. 123]

And in that "search" for the knives, on their separate paths, they both vomit shamefully. Let us note the inversion in the two books: on the positive side—the knights—the balsam has a healthful effect only on Don Quixote; on the negative side—the pirates—tobacco, a pirate's trademark, sets well only with Huck, who is al-

ready hardened in the vice. As far as I know, this point
has never been examined either. But what is important
is the following: aren't we seeing here, too, how much
there is in Don Quixote of "childish things"?

Let us go on to another point. One night the master
and servant find themselves with nothing to eat and no
place to sleep.

And to complete their distress, they had an adventure that,
without any contrivance at all, really appeared to be one.
[P. 179]

And so it happens:

[They] saw coming toward them . . . a great number of
lights. . . . Sancho stood aghast at the sight of them, and
Don Quixote himself felt uneasy. The former pulled at the
halter of his ass, the latter at the reins of his horse, and
both stood peering earnestly in front of them and wonder-
ing what it could be. They saw that the lights were advanc-
ing toward them and that as they approached nearer and
nearer, they became bigger and bigger. At the sight of
them Sancho began to tremble like one with quicksilver
poisoning, and Don Quixote's hair stood on end. [P. 179]

Then we see that this is the adventure of the corpse.
And Don Quixote, who had felt the shivers of something supernatural sweep over him, masters himself like
the knight that he is, he attacks and he conquers.

Sancho, meanwhile, had been watching the fight, amazed
at the boldness of his master, and he said to himself: "This
master of mine is surely as strong and brave as he says."
[P. 181]

which shows that, at other times, Sancho had been in
doubt. But this is not the important point about this

part; once again we must look at this passage from the perspective of *Tom Sawyer*. Who does not remember the night when Tom and Huck go to the cemetery with their dead cat, looking for "adventures," and there, "without any contrivance at all," they watch nothing less than a real murder.

In this case I do not want to point out the game aspect as much as I do the literary material in the two texts: through them a game is made of the adventures; but, so that the reader will not feel disappointed, a real adventure must be inserted from time to time. And in this sense, the "without any contrivance at all" becomes a real piece of enlightenment, for it is as much as to say that in the other adventures, in those that we shall call "adventures," there really is some contrivance. And since one of Cervantes' famous winks is in this, we should comment on it. The adventures that have a "contrivance" are precisely those that are generally termed "realistic." That is, Don Quixote looks for adventures, and he gets a beating. But this one, where there is no contrivance, is the kind that holds an element of mystery, of an unrealistic true adventure—at least in its beginning. And the contrivance comes after the fact, when we finally know the feasible and plausible character of it all—after we have been enticed by a shiver of fright. So then, do we not see almost exactly the same thing in *Tom Sawyer* in the cemetery scene that we have already spoken about? Or in everything about the treasure hunt? It will be remembered that Tom has convinced Huck that "treasures" are "out there," just waiting for someone to find them. They make several attempts, but the treasure does not turn up. Tom thinks that next to an old abandoned house will be a good place. They go there and look around. And it so happens that while they are playing at "hunting for treasure," they hear a noise, they hide, and none other than Injun Joe—the murderer at the cemetery— shows up, with a comrade. And finally, with the hidden and terrified boys watching, they uncover from the floor of the cabin a real treasure. In spite of their terror, Tom and Huck decide to recover "their" treasure— which finally happens at the end of the book, and according to all the "rules" that Tom could desire for such matters: under mysterious conditions, at the foot of a cross, with puzzling inscriptions, in a cave, and so on.

Now let us look at part of what takes place on the Sierra Morena. I am referring to the finding of the portmanteau. At his master's command, Sancho looks and finds "a little heap of gold crowns," and then, "after further searching he found a little memorandum book richly bound. Don Quixote asked him for this, but told him to keep the money for himself."

Let us pause for a moment with this encounter. It is evident that, for Sancho (who is incapable of inventing the "game," but has a real desire to play it) if all the adventures were of a negative nature, the supposed realism of the book would demand that at some time he finally learn from experience and abandon his master. On the other hand, the reader himself needs to feel some excitement of adventure—since there is so much talk about it—and that appetite must be satisfied. This, I think, is one of the main reasons why we have Tom Sawyer finding the treasure. In other words, both Cervantes and Mark Twain realized they could not look for adventure all the time, and never have one.

Getting back to the main theme, Don Quixote's letter is introduced here. When he sees the verses in the little book, and inasmuch as the knight speaks well of them, Sancho asks him if he knows how to write poetry too:

"And better than you think," answered Don Quixote, **"as you shall see when you take a letter, written in verse from beginning to end, to my Lady Dulcinea of El Toboso."** [P. 223]

The story of that letter has been masterfully studied by Pedro Salinas, and therefore I would have only to quote his study, if it were not for just one thing: if we transcribed on these pages that type of "realm of the absurd" that Salinas sees in his work, I believe that it could very well appear to be corroborating my game theory. Let us summarize a part of the whole affair. Don Quixote writes a letter to Dulcinea—even though he realizes that she does not know how to read or write; the letter lies forgotten in the little memorandum book—and Don Quixote is not unaware of the fact; Sancho does not go to El Toboso, and so he does not see Dulcinea either. Under these circumstances there arises the dialogue between Sancho—who is aggressive in making up lies about one reality—and Don Quixote—who invents another reality that decidedly opposes Sancho's. Let us make a summary of what happens:

"Did you find her stringing pearls?" "No, she was winnowing bushels of wheat." "Was it the white sort?" "No, it was red." "Did you not perceive an aromatic fragrance, something sweet?" "I got a whiff of something a bit mannish; this must have been . . . because she was sweating." "What did she do when she read the letter?" [Pp. 311–312]

Sancho's answer to that must be put down in toto:

She did not read it . . . for she said she could neither read nor write. She tore it up into tiny pieces, saying that she did not wish to give it to anybody to read for fear her secrets might be known all over the village. She said it was enough to hear what I had told her by word of mouth about your love for her. [P. 312]

That is, even while Sancho is lying, he has put it all back together without meaning to, and of course without knowing, when he says "it was enough." "It was enough," really, for Don Quixote to have a pretext to go on, no matter how small it might be. To go on doing what? Obviously, and this is what I find important here, to go on playing: the part of a gallant here, the part of a knight forever.

Notice another point: the penance that Don Quixote performs in imitation of Amadís. When Sancho tries to understand the reasons for this penance, and asks:

What signs have you discovered that her ladyship, Dulcinea of El Toboso, has committed any foolishness either with Moor or Christian? [P. 242]

Don Quixote replies with the well-known words:

That is just the point of it . . . and that is where the subtleness of my plan comes in. A knight-errant who goes mad for a good reason deserves no thanks or gratitude; the whole point consists in going crazy without cause, and thereby warn my lady what to expect from me in the wet if this is what I do in the dry. [P. 242]

Now let us look at the reasoning of Tom Sawyer. Huck, moved by an unspoken feeling of Christian brotherhood, has undertaken to free the Negro, Jim, rashly and without any plan at all. But when Tom arrives, he immediately shows his friend the need for such a plan. Each of the boys makes up his own scheme, and they compare them to see which is better. After Huck has revealed his idea, he asks: "Wouldn't that plan work?" Tom answers:

> *Work?* Why, cert'nly it would work, like rats a-fighting. But it's too blame' simple; there ain't nothing *to* it. What's the good of a plan that ain't no more trouble than that? It's as mild as goosemilk. Why, Huck, it wouldn't make no more talk than breaking into a soap factory. [P. 522]

That is, Tom wants to do "crazy things in the dry," so that people can see what he would do in the wet. They have to free Jim, of course, but at the same time they have to do something more. What? Something that is not easy; something that goes along with the books: in a word, imitate the penance of Amadís.

Let us get back to Don Quixote. As soon as the time comes to do "crazy things in the dry," he finds it necessary to write the famous letter, about which Don Quixote says:

> and since we have no paper, we should write as the ancients did on leaves of trees or on tablets of wax. [P. 247]

Tom Sawyer's own wish is that Jim write "messages" on the prison wall; but since this "dungeon" does not have stone walls—which is the proper element for such messages (one of which we saw earlier)—Tom comes up with the ideal solution: the grindstone from the mill, so the message can really be written the way required by the canons—that is, Tom's books of chivalry. They have to free Jim: agreed. But they have to do it Tom's way. The essential thing is that Jim has to "suffer," "to be chained," "to inscribe messages on stone," and in some way he has to do what Don Quixote did, following "the ancients."

Stepping back now to see all this from a greater distance, I do not think Don Quixote would have been able to play his game without some material support for it. So then, if we consider the book in its entirety, we see that there seem to be two types of characters: some we will call simply "literary"—Luscinda, Lela Marien— and others we will call Cervantian by definition—Don Quixote and Sancho as well as Sansón Carrasco, the Curate, the Barber—who are more "realistic" types. But the fact is there are some characters who are simultaneously Cervantian and also Don Quixotian. Just one example of this type will be enough for us to see more clearly what I want to point out: Dorotea—Princess Micomicona.

As the reader will recall, there is a chapter that deals with "the pleasant device" to rescue Don Quixote from his "severe penance." The device consists of a young lady asking Don Quixote for help and protection. Dorotea offers to "become" Princess Micomicona—which turns out to be especially valid proof for Don Quixote. And the really choice item of the game, Sancho's credulity when the Curate introduces the girl to him as a princess. Let us see how Sancho Panza licks his lips in delight:

Happy search makes happy finds . . . especially if my master has the luck to undo the wrongs by wiping out the whoreson giant . . . ; kill him he surely will . . . unless he turns out to be a ghost. [P. 292]

If, to that, we add the fact that this same Micomicona "threw herself on her knees before Don Quixote,"

it is not difficult to see why the knight has another attack of enthusiast virtue:

**I do vouchsafe and grant it to you . . . provided it be noth-
ing detrimental to my king, my country, or to her who
keeps the key of my heart and liberty. [P. 294]**

What more could Don Quixote ask for? Everyone is
trying to deceive him with that "pleasant device"; but it
so happens they all succeed in entrenching him firmly
in his game. But observe carefully that Dorotea, the
character, is "real," has her own life, loves, and so on;
but now, for Don Quixote, she becomes a character out
of another novel—one that the Curate invents to deceive Don Quixote, or better yet, one from Don Quixote himself—a novel in action. This process of mixing
one fiction with another has the effect of giving things
and situations a realistic appearance for Don Quixote,
who is a pure soul, so that he can go on playing his
game without any scruples of credence. But what happens in the American book—or books? Tom and Huck
are Mark Twain's novel. Injun Joe (a real murderer,
whose crime the boys fortuitously witnessed) and the
Negro Jim, on the one hand, are "real," true characters
of Mark Twain; but on the other hand they are—as far
as Tom and Huck themselves are concerned—characters from their own novel, from their game. For, around
them, Tom and Huck can make their own creative imag-
inings come true, in a feasible and plausible way.

Let us go back a little now, to see the intrigue that
precedes the episode with Micomicona. The Curate
and the Barber come out of the inn with their companions. The Barber is disguised with a false beard. When
they come upon Don Quixote, the Curate pretends to

recognize him, and after greetings are exchanged, Cervantes arranges for one of the mules to give a couple of kicks, and as a result:

[the Barber] fell to the ground with so little care for his beard that it fell off. Finding himself without it, he could find no other remedy than to cover his face with both hands and cry out that his grinders were stove in. [P. 297]

But Don Quixote examines this occurrence with the same "sharpness of perception" that Dostoevski attributes to Myshkin. And so, by his very words, we see that Don Quixote says nothing about grinders, but he does say something about beards:

Don Quixote, seeing that huge mass of beard without jaws or blood lying a good distance away from the fallen squire's face, exclaimed: "By the living God, this is a great miracle! His beard has been wrenched and torn clean off his face as if he had been shaved." [P. 297]

We are then told how the Curate saw the danger and fixed the beard back on the Barber's face, pretending to say a charm "for sticking on beards":

Don Quixote was dumbfounded at what he saw, and he begged the curate to teach him that charm when he had the time. . . . [and the curate] promised to explain it to him at the first opportunity. [Pp. 297-298]

But how is it that when confronted by such a thing, a "magical" thing, Don Quixote does not insist? And, furthermore, why does Cervantes insist on piling up such ordinary material difficulties like this one about the beard? Would it have been less plausible to ignore all this, taking it for granted that Don Quixote did not recognize the Barber? But that is where Cervantes is winking: when he shows us these coarse jokes which Don Quixote recognizes for what they are—"as if he had been shaved"—so that the inner truth of the character can stand exposed to us. This truth consists of making us see that Don Quixote is aware of the trick (and for that purpose, Cervantes makes it so gross an occurrence that it would not fool anyone), so that Don Quixote can reveal himself. And it is my belief that Cervantes' wink is in the way the knight reveals himself: Don Quixote is aware of the trick, but he does not want to be aware of it.

But very quickly—after the battle with the wineskins —everything becomes much more subtle. Sancho, after one of his "falls" discovers that there is no giant, and no princess, and so he tells his master: "everything is finished." Don Quixote replies that he can easily believe that, and he mentions the blood that ran in streams "just like water." And Sancho says:

Like red wine . . . I want to tell you, your worship . . . that your dead giant is no other than a slashed wineskin, that the blood is a dozen gallons of red wine . . . and that the cutoff head is the whore that bore me. [P. 381]

We might expect another outburst because of such uncivil words, and especially because of the disrespect they imply; however, Don Quixote now appears strangely benign before such "blasphemy" (there is no giant and no princess):

What are you saying, you mad fool? . . . Are you in your senses? [P. 381]

Master and servant go looking for proof. But Dorotea, who meanwhile has returned to her role as Micomi-

cona, assures him that she is still the princess. And
when Sancho (thanks to Micomicona's intervention)
takes back his previous irreverence, Don Quixote again
gives the stock answers, which his American grandson
has learned so well:

**I now say, Sancho . . . you are a blockhead, but pardon
me. We have had enough of this. [P. 384]**

Above all: "We have had enough of this." That is the
important thing: to leave the matter there—so that the
other matter, the really important one, will go on. Do
we not see this much more clearly with that "numskull," coming from Tom Sawyer? Furthermore, with
his pure heart Don Quixote nearly comes to the point
of telling us as much in one of his bursts of enthusiasm:

**Who would say that this lady by my side is the great queen
we all know her to be and that I am that Knight of the
Rueful Figure so celebrated abroad by the mouth of Fame?
Now there can be no doubt . . . [P. 387]**

We are facing a superlative case of magic, since it is
so magical it makes doubt disappear even in Don Quixote himself. But if this is a crowning point regarding
Don Quixote, there is another key point in the First
Part regarding Cervantes, for now he is going to tell us
something clearly, without being evasive, when he
mentions "a certain Saavedra." Remembering Algiers—
a true basis for Don Quixote—the captive tells us that
he "had attempted in a thousand ways to escape":

**for I never abandoned the hope of obtaining my liberty.
When in my plots and schemes and attempts the result
did not come up to my expectations, I never gave way to
despair, but pretended and at once I began to devise some**

new hope to support me, however faint or feeble it might be. [P. 403]

Since this is a major occurrence, it will be worth our while to examine it closely. If we call to mind the theory of outrage on the soul, we obviously cannot help relating Saavedra's words to that sinister specter of an execution that Dostoevski had to go through. That is why there exists that conviction, that feeling of something lived through, which is passed on to the reader through Myshkin's words. I believe the basis for the theme of liberty in Cervantes is no different. And when I say this, I am, of course, not proposing any sort of determinism: these same experiences, had anyone other than Dostoevski or Cervantes gone through them, would not have produced these two matchless books. But when we remember Cervantes' actions in the bagnios of Algiers, with his real enthusiasm for heroic virtue, we see, with the same evidence that exists in Dostoevski's case, how much of personal experience there is in the anxiety for liberty which runs throughout this work of Cervantes. That is why the lines quoted above constitute a real confidence on Cervantes' part—in regard to "his" outrage on the soul—with that statement, "I pretended and at once I began to devise some new hope . . . however faint and feeble it might be." But on the other hand, this "pretended": is this not really the key to Don Quixote—not to Cervantes—with its touch of the ridiculous too? And is all this not something that a child—any child—will do? Or do we need something more to definitely link Don Quixote, Tom Sawyer, and Myshkin as brothers?

Keeping all this in mind, let us see how the outrage on the soul comes about for Don Quixote—not for Cervantes. As we will recall, at a certain point the Curate, the Barber, Dorotea, and the others, are at the inn. And finally they "entered the room where [Don Quixote] lay sleeping" and they tied him up:

so that when he awoke with a start he could not move. . . . And straightaway his . . . imagination suggested to him that these were the phantoms of that enchanted castle and that without any doubt he was enchanted, for he could neither move nor defend himself. [P. 468]

That is, the enchantment is used as a pretext to have hope: hope that Cervantes never lost, and when it was absent, when he had no other recourse, he pretended. Therefore, when Don Quixote understands things as they really are, he pretends, in his own way, and he is astonished that they are not carrying him through the air:

To be carried off in an oxcart! By the living God, it fills me with shame! Perhaps, however, the chivalries and enchantments of our day follow a different road from that followed by the ancients. [P. 471]

And while they are traveling this way—according to the new style of enchantments: in a cage, hands tied, in complete silence—some men come along on horseback. They want to know what is happening, and Don Quixote—melancholy, but lucid—says:

Are you gentlemen, perchance, well versed and skilled in matters of knight-errantry? If you are, I will communicate my misfortunes to you; if not, there is no reason why I should weary myself relating them. [P. 474]

It is obvious that if they are not "skilled," they will not understand him. What adult could seriously expect a child to "communicate" his troubles to him? But as soon as the others mollify him about their knowledge of chivalresque things, we see Don Quixote speaking clearly while at the same time maintaining the magic among the initiated:

I am traveling in this cage under a spell because of the envy and treachery of evil enchanters. [P. 475]

And when the Curate pretends to back up Don Quixote's reasoning, Sancho shows that he knows full well what the others are up to. But although he does not know how to create the game like his master, he does know how to follow him perfectly. Therefore, he, so credulous at other times, exclaims: "Don Quixote is no more enchanted than my mother." And to back up his assertion, he mentions his master's physical needs as proof—which could not be more conclusive—and then he turns to the Curate:

O Master Curate, Master Curate. Do you think I don't recognize you? And do you imagine that I don't spot what you're up to and that I don't see through these newfangled enchantments? Of course I know you, even though you've a mask on your face. . . . Bad luck to the Devil! If it were not for your reverence, by this time my master would have been married to the Infanta Micomicona, and I'd have been a count. [P. 476]

Notice, in the first place, that Sancho is talking about the "Infanta Micomicona," even though he was the one who discovered the deceit (she is not the Infanta because she is "nuzzling with somebody of the present company"). How do we explain this? When he replies to the Barber, Sancho himself gives us an answer that is more than sufficient. At the Barber's reproaches ("That

was an unlucky hour when you became impregnated
with his promises, and . . . that island you crave.")
Sancho, after replying that he is "not in child by anyone," also speaks clearly:

**and if I'm set on getting islands, others are set on worse.
. . . Mind how you speak, Master Barber, for shaving
beards is not all, and there is a great difference between
Pedro and Pedro. . . . As to this business of enchanting my
master, God knows the truth. [Pp. 476–477]**

Notice that these are words that let us see a Sancho
who seems to know exactly what kind of "islands" he is
looking for and what kind of enchantment his master is
under—and, even while knowing this, he not only does
not renounce the whole business but, on the contrary,
affirms it as something better: "others are set on
worse."

That is, now—as in the Second Part—the attitudes
are reversed. We have before us a Sancho who wants to
go on playing—but who is incapable of making up the
game—and a melancholy Don Quixote who is looking
for a special and final refuge in his magical inner
world. So, when the squire keeps insisting that his master is not enchanted, Don Quixote, even while he accepts Sancho's arguments, holds onto a refuge for himself, his inner world:

**So, there is no use arguing against custom. . . . I know,
and I am convinced, that I am enchanted, and that is
enough for the peace of my conscience. If I were not enchanted, I would be greatly perturbed to think that I had
let myself be cooped up in this cage. [P. 488]**

Subjectivism is certainly the only refuge when objec-
tivity intolerably harasses us. But later, when the

knight asserts the positive qualities he has taken on ever since he became a knight-errant ("Valient, courteous, liberal," etc.), he adds:

And although it is so short a while since I found myself shut up in a cage like a madman . . . [P. 498]

And that, we might say, is another of Cervantes' famous winks, for up to now we were not told Don Quixote knew they were taking him along like a madman, since, shortly before, his historian gave us some words about "his conscience." And the contradiction here is important, since it gives us the ambivalence of the thinking—the real "double-thinking"—of Don Quixote: when he is with Sancho in the magic world, he knows in his conscience that he is enchanted; but when completely caught up in the game itself, he reaches a point where he forgets about details, and he himself tells us that he knows they are taking him along like a madman. Could it be stated more clearly?

After the fight with the goatherd who dares take him for a madman, Don Quixote goes up to the disciplinants who are carrying an image of the "most blessed Immaculate Virgin." As soon as he sees the tears of the "lady," the knight, of course, wants to free her. And as if the drudging that the goatherd had given him were not enough, now the disciplinants trounce him, leaving him so badly beaten that Sancho weeps, thinking he has been killed. In the midst of Sancho's cries, the knight not only revives but, when he sees himself understood—intimately—by his squire, we might say that Don Quixote "comes back to life"—although now it is to a very melancholy life:

He who lives absent from thee, sweet Dulcinea, endures far greater sufferings than these. Help me, friend Sancho, to lift myself into the enchanted cart, for I am no longer in a condition to press the saddle of Rocinante. [P. 512]

Words full of mystery. On the one hand, Sancho makes him "come back to life" and be Don Quixote once more; but on the other hand, the very same Don Quixote sees himself under such circumstances as to ask for the cage—magically converted into an "enchanted cart." If it were a vulgar oxcart fixed up as a cage for a madman, it would be intolerable. But all that is necessary is to enchant the cart, and now everything is the way it must be—in his conscience.

On the surface, in that most bitter of endings of the First Part, I do not think there is any doubt about Cervantes' intention of alluding, in some way, to the Passion of Our Lord: such is the sarcasm and contempt with which he makes Don Quixote enter his village:

They made their entrance at noon, and as it happened to be Sunday, all the people were in the marketplace when the wagon passed through. . . . A boy ran off at full speed to give the news to his housekeeper and his niece that their master and uncle was coming home lean and yellow, stretched out on a bundle of hay in an oxcart. [Pp. 512–513]

Does all this not call to mind the scourging, the purple cloak, the vinegar? But was Dostoevski not actually one of the first—if not the first—to see how much there is of Christ in Don Quixote? And was he not also the first to appreciate this book as "the most beautiful work in all of Christian literature"—but clarifying his thought when he adds: "because it is also ridiculous"?

I think that the final counterpoint of this First Part is in Sancho's words to his wife. When she asks what is all this about islands, he answers, "Honey is not for an ass's mouth," words that are more mysterious than insolent, since they tend to preserve the occult science he has learned with his master, the magic, the mystery: the island. And, furthermore, when he tells about his adventures, he adds that "there's nothing in the world so pleasant" since, even though he often comes out battered:

when all's said and done, it's a fine thing to be gadding about spying for chances, crossing mountains, exploring woods. . . . lodging in inns at our own sweet will, with devil a maravedi to pay. [P. 514]

In other words, Huck Finn already knows that when all is said and done, you're better off following Tom, since, besides enchanted things, there are sometimes real treasures that only Tom would have known how to find.

What Sancho does not know yet is that he is going to rise even higher: for if Huck and Tom found their treasure, their grandfather became governor of an island.

4

The Second Part of
Don Quixote

Perhaps what is most characteristic about the Second
Part of *Don Quixote* is that the distinction between
Don Quixote's sanity and his insanity becomes much
more nebulous, and in a very subtle way. There is nothing here that resembles the windmills, the wineskins,
or the cage used to take him back to his village. And
also, everything is much more feasible and plausible
now that Don Quixote almost always has material support—outside of himself—which backs up his inner
world. Sansón Carrasco makes his appearance as a
rival knight. The Duke and Duchess treat Don Quixote
the way he knows a knight should be treated. There is
nothing implausible now, specifically, other than the
episode in the Cave of Montesinos.

According to Cide Hamete, a month has gone by
since Don Quixote arrived at the village in the "en-

chanted cart." At the end of this time, everyone came
to believe "that he was quite recovered and in full possession of his wits." The Curate then decides to make
the decisive test: "to touch on the subject of chivalry,"
telling him that "the Turk was descending" and speaking to him about his Majesty's provisions. How will
Don Quixote react? And here we have the first demonstration of Cervantes' style for the Second Part: Don
Quixote—for the first time in his life—appears cautious
and reserved:

**His Majesty has acted like a most prudent warrior . . .
but if he would take my advice, I would counsel him to
take one precaution of which His Majesty is not aware.
[P. 530]**

I think this great caution shows that Don Quixote
has not forgotten the enchanted cart. Moreover, his
caution is immediately justified when the Barber insin-
uates that perhaps the Quixotic advice might be added
to "the long list of unpractical projects usually offered
to princes." And Don Quixote replies violently:

**Mine, Mr. Scrapebeard, are not unpractical but highly
practical. [P. 530]**

This gives excellent proof of his complete faculties
for knowing that "two can play at this game": at the
duplicity of his friends, he first shows caution; at their
aggressive malice, he becomes violently defensive. All
this proves that he is aware. But just because he is
aware, he does not give up. He talks about the advice
he would give the king: to call on the knights-errant.
And when the Barber delivers his story about madmen,
since "it fits this situation like a glove," telling about a

madman who believed he was Neptune, Don Quixote, after rebuking him again ("Master Scrapebeard"), gives the final answer to this point:

Therefore I wish to remain at home, since the chaplain is not taking me out, and if Jupiter, as the Barber has said, will not rain, here am I who will rain whenever I please. This I say so that Master Basin may see that I understand him. [P. 536]

That is, from the very first moment, Cervantes puts us back into the sanity-insanity option, affirming that his character is crazy, but at the same time letting us see that he really is not. And while he showed this with the broken helmet in the First Part, he now does it by means of this dialogue in which Don Quixote appears very reserved, but not so much so that he would not put the Barber in his place three consecutive times ("Scrapebeard," "Master Scrapebeard," "Master Basin"). The Curate escapes because of his cloth. And all this occurs without Don Quixote, even for a moment, renouncing his game: "God understands me."

But if the idea continues in basically the same way, we will see that, beginning with the second chapter, a new factor enters which simultaneously builds up the reality of the character and the "magic reality" of his game. Even though Sancho is "announced"—let us say —by means of a discussion with the Housekeeper, Don Quixote, contrary to what might be expected from a madman, is very uneasy. And we are not told this obliquely but clearly:

afraid Sancho would blurt out a whole heap of mischievous nonsense and touch upon points that might not be wholly to his credit. [P. 540]

What "points" could those be, if Don Quixote were really crazy? Let us switch to Tom Sawyer. So that Tom cannot go swimming in the Mississippi, Aunt Polly sews together the neck of his shirt every day. As a result, Tom has to take it apart and sew it back together again everytime he swims in the river. Then Sid, Tom's half brother, exposes the game by intruding in his usual sensible way. (Again notice the inversion that Mark Twain introduces into a Cervantian situation.) And now let us look at the scene:

"Tom, you didn't have to undo your shirt-collar where I sewed it, to pump on your head, did you? Unbutton your jacket!"
The trouble vanished out of Tom's face. He opened his jacket. His shirt-collar was securely sewed.
"Bother! Well, go 'long with you. I'd made sure you'd played hookey and been a-swimming. But I forgive ye, Tom. I reckon you're a kind of a singed cat, as the saying is—better'n you look. *This time*." . . .
But Sidney said:
"Well, now, if I didn't think you sewed his collar with white thread, but it's black."
"Why, I did sew it with white! Tom!"
But Tom did not wait for the rest. As he went out at the door he said:
"Siddy, I'll lick you for that!" [P. 10]

Another point about "genealogical" evidence which I believe has been overlooked. And yet I do not think Tom's fear of his aunt could be any more closely linked to Don Quixote's fear of his niece.

Let us get back to Don Quixote and Sancho. After Sancho's noisy arrival, Don Quixote "shut himself in his room with Sancho"—getting away from witnesses: Aunt Polly. But do they shut themselves in together to talk about enchantments? Not at all: but to make re-

proaches. Don Quixote reprimands Sancho for going
around saying that his master "took him from his cot-
tage"; Sancho, on the defensive, talks about the blan-
keting he got—knowing very well that this is a sensi-
tive point for Don Quixote and his guilty conscience. In
any event, this is a case of being secretive when with
adults or their equivalents: the Sids. Why, if Don Quixote is a madman?

But that was something that appeared in the First
Part. What is new here is that after this "scene," we see
Don Quixote's consciousness of his own existence objec-
tified before the others:

> **But let us put that aside. . . . Now tell me Sancho, my
> friend, what do they say about me in that place? What
> opinion of me have the common people? [P. 541]**

First let us notice the depreciatory—defensive—
tone: "that place," before knowing what "the common
people" were thinking. And when Sancho cooperates
by informing him—"mad but droll," "valiant but unfortunate," and so on, it is Cervantes now—not just Don
Quixote—who creates the magic that culminates in the
appearance of Sansón Carrasco. And he becomes the
artistic key for the Second Part since he substantiates
Don Quixote's "game." He is, if you wish, the "anti-
Quixote" par excellence; but because of this, he turns
out to be the shadow that accentuates the stature of
the real one. Among other reasons, because after this
moment—and thanks to this character—Don Quixote
knows that his game has become real. For during the
secret meeting, Sancho tells his master about the *History of the Ingenious Gentleman,* which the squire
knows of thanks to the Bachelor.

But although Don Quixote "could not convince him-

self that such a history could exist," the Bachelor himself then arrives and confirms the news, not in an ordinary way, but "dropping to his knees before Don Quixote." When the latter answers, he lets us see the es-
sence of his inner world.

**So it is true that there is a history of me and that it was a
Moor and a wise man who wrote it? [P. 545]**

This is an utterly childlike question that contains a
sense of total awe at seeing that dreams—"games"—become real. This knight who, we are told, took inns for
castles, cannot be convinced even of a simple truth
now. I do not think there has ever been a child who
has not had something similar happen to him. There is
one I know of whose father was a hunter: One night he
was awakened and a gun was put in his hands—for
him; and thinking it was a toy, it all seemed like a
dream to him. But when he realized that it was real, he
could not believe what he saw with his own eyes, since
before he had gotten the gun, he had "killed" thou-
sands of animals he could really believe in—and believe in firmly. As for Don Quixote, he has barely recovered from his surprise when he asks:

**but tell me, Master Bachelor, which of my deeds are most
highly praised in this history? [P. 546]**

Here are words that, since they take for granted that
there is a history and deeds too, make Don Quixote appear as a person unexpectedly caught up in his own
world of magic. If he was "playing" in the First Part,
he does not stop now; but now it is with a look of awe
at the world of mystery, seeing that his games have
been changed into reality. Up to this moment he was

certainly making his assertions, but all the while he
knew; now, however, it happens that "there is a true
history" and a "sage" who composed it and everything.
This, in a major key, is something like what happens in
a minor key to Sancho—the "enchanter" of Dulcinea—
when he later "becomes enchanted" himself. In short,
there will be a game now, just as there was before, but
there will be something more too.

Before examining the appearance of this character,
Sansón Carrasco, with all its importance, let us note
that his presence alone is like a real shot of assurance
for Don Quixote. And it is so potent that it is magically
carried over to his squire. Let us look at the chapter
that the "translator" believes is apocryphal becomes of
Sancho's way of speaking. It is true that the squire's
speech is somewhat lofty at times. One of these is when
he replies to his wife, who has asked him why he is
looking so happy:

**Wife, if God were willing, I'd be very glad to be less merry
than I am this instant. [P. 557]**

And in another passage, after he has announced his decision to set out again with Don Quixote, and his wife
does not understand him:

**It is enough if God understands me, wife . . . for it's no
wedding we are going to, but around the world to engage
in the game of give-and-take with giants and dragons and
monsters. [P. 558]**

This is, of course, a clear case of contagion from his
master's language. But let us look at that same situation
through Tom Sawyer. Or to be more precise, through
Huck Finn. How does Huck talk to the Negro, Jim?

Does he not actually become condescending and talk to him "from above"—exactly the way he is used to listening to Tom?

I never see such a nigger. If he got a notion in his head once, there warn't no getting it out again. . . . So I went to talking about other kings, and let Solomon slide. I told about Louis Sixteenth that got his head cut off in France . . . and about his little boy the dolphin . . . and some say he died there [in jail].

"Po' little chap."

"But some says he got out . . . and come to America." [P. 346]

They debate what the Dolphin might have been able to do in America—since "dey ain' no kings here"—and they get to the point where Huck tells Jim that some get on the police force, and "some of them learns people how to talk French." And when Jim is astonished that the French do not speak like everyone else, Huck assures him that if a person did not know French, he would not be able to understand a single word. Jim gives a disgusted reply to that, and asks how that could be. And Huck:

I don't know; but it's so. I got some of their jabber out of a book. S'pose a man was to come to you and say Polly-voo-franzy—what would you think? [P. 346]

Is this dialogue between Huck and Jim actually not a replica—although a superficial one—of the numerous talks Tom and Huck have had? And is there not really an obvious parallel in both situations to the familiar ones, first between Don Quixote and Sancho, and then Sancho and Teresa? And yet, I do not think that historical French lesson Huck gives to Jim has ever been examined.

We are now going to see a conflict of internal politics for Don Quixote. Teresa Panza persuades her husband to ask for a salary. And from Teresa's persuasive powers comes one of the few deceits between the master and his squire, concerning who would be Don Quixote's squire if Sancho would no longer accompany him, as he is threatening to do. And this is when the Bachelor, Sansón Carrasco, enters and offers himself as a squire. If the Bachelor was important before for having brought the news about the *History*, now, when he can contest Sancho's "strike," he rises greatly in Don Quixote's esteem:

Did I not tell you, Sancho, that there would be squires in plenty? Take note that he who offers his services is no other than the renowned bachelor Sansón Carrasco. [P. 574]

"Renowned": to be sure. For in a way, this character is the "motor" that Cervantes has had the insight to put into the Second Part, because now by means of him everything will indeed become true. That is why the above words are followed by so many different eulogies: enough to break the corporate will—not just of Sancho, but of all corporations put together.

The historian begins chapter viii with exclamations of joy for "finding that he has already got Don Quixote and Sancho Panza into the field," that is, because he can show us Don Quixote in his own element: liberty. Material liberty—with respect to Aunt Polly—and spiritual liberty to play the game the niece spoke of shortly before, without understanding it, and that consists of "being valiant when you are old," and so forth.

They have barely gotten away from the house and the niece when Don Quixote decides to go to El Toboso before getting involved in another adventure. And, as if nothing had happened at all in the entire First Part, we see that Don Quixote abandons all care and continues what he was doing before he had been brought back in the enchanted cart. To begin with, the fencing between Don Quixote and Sancho over Dulcinea is continued. Don Quixote asserts what Dulcinea should be and therefore is, without letting himself be intimidated by Sancho's concocted reality about his trip to El Toboso ("winnowing wheat—stringing pearls"). Right now let us listen to Don Quixote's decisive argument:

What! Do you still insist . . . that . . . Dulcinea was winnowing wheat—a task and occupation utterly at variance with what is done and should be done by ladies of rank? [P. 578]

These words are the signal to begin the game now— a signal for the initiated, of course. So Don Quixote immediately launches into an erudite declamation about fame, for Sancho's benefit:

What was it, do you think, that drove Horatius . . . to cast himself down from the bridge . . . ? And to come down to more modern times, what scuttled the ships and left the valiant Spaniards, led by the most courteous Cortés, isolated in the New World? [Pp. 580–581]

It was fame, of course, in Don Quixote's opinion. But here it is important to notice that one of the prototypes the knight refers to, Cortés, was a real and contemporary Spaniard. Could it be stated more clearly that Don Quixote is playing at being Cortés? At any rate, his example is sufficient to make his squire—also an echo of contemporary reality in Spain—oppose his master in a debate of the best sort: "Which is the greater thing: to bring a dead man to life or to kill a giant?" And as Don Quixote agrees—"The answer is obvious"—Sancho concludes very logically:

that we might set about becoming saints. Then we shall get the good name we're after all the sooner. [Pp. 582–583]

In Sancho's reply is an important point for my thesis. Saintliness is important to Sancho for fame at the very most. But over and above this, could we seriously believe that Sancho would do anything practical toward becoming a saint? From his lips, this is nothing more than sophistry against his master—but that is from his master's perspective. If Don Quixote is playing at being Cortés, Sancho continues the game—verbally—showing that there is an even greater fame; but he does it only on the pretext of a debate in order to go on playing. That is, Don Quixote is playing, from within, at being Cortés, while Sancho, from without, verbally plays at being even more—which is a way of giving in to Don Quixote's game.

Let us continue along the road to El Toboso. The author of the book puts Don Quixote in a highly tense situation here. The supposed focal point of all of Don Quixote's impulses is Dulcinea—who lives, and yet does not live, in El Toboso. While the hero was far away, clichés about enchantment were sufficient. But now that he is right here, in this very town, the risk is much greater for any magic.

In El Toboso now, and with things going badly for the squire because of his lies, Sancho has to become ethical. He says that they should not look for Dulcinea at this hour as if they were visiting "the houses of our wenches." Finally, Sancho says that "if I remember right," the lady's house is "in a blind alley," and his master replies, saying that such a thing has no precedent in affairs of chivalry. And Sancho, seeing that he is trapped, says that he does not remember very well since he was here only once, thereby giving Don Quixote a reason to tell us something remarkable:

Look here, you heretic; have I not told you a thousand times that never once in my life have I seen the peerless Dulcinea, nor have I ever crossed the threshold of her palace? I am enamoured only by hearsay. [P. 585]

In the first place, this version is contradictory to what we are told about Aldonza Lorenzo and whether or not she had a "good hand at salting pork." But what is most important is that Don Quixote now asserts that he is "enamoured only by hearsay." In other words, he is playing at being in love as a complement to his game of playing "Cortés." Aside from this, what are the master and servant going to do in El Toboso this night? A critical moment for the entire book, which Sancho astutely resolves, with the even more astute and subtle collaboration of Don Quixote himself. Sancho, who "was in a fever to get his master out of the village," suggests:

the day will be soon upon us. . . . It will be better for us to leave the city and . . . hide in some neighboring wood, and I'll return by day and search in every corner for the house, castle, or palace of my lady. [P. 587]

These are words that, despite all Sancho's cautious skirting ("house, castle or palace") could not be any more like making him eat humble pie than they already are. That is, no one could stomach those words except a person who, like Don Quixote, has decided "to swallow them" as well as he can. Let us see how the knight does it:

Sancho . . . you have uttered a thousand words of wisdom in a few brief sentences. I willingly accept the advice you have given me. Come on, son, let us look for a place where I may hide. [P. 587]

Notice that he takes Sancho's advice "willingly." Does this not seem odd? He finds himself at the very place where the woman of his dreams lives; the "castle" should be close by; he has just said that he has never seen his lady and now that he is on the point of being able to see her, at precisely this moment, he takes the advice—to leave—willingly. It would not be possible in this case either, to say more clearly what Don Quixote is thinking—and quite sanely. That is why he cannot be the one to take the initiative, and that is why, when Sancho takes it—for his own reasons—Don Quixote accepts the advice willingly. So Sancho achieves his goal: to deceive Don Quixote. But he achieves his goal thanks to the very subtle collaboration of Don Quixote himself who accepts the deceit willingly.

Now let us take a look at the Adventure of the Parliament of Death. Notice after the usual ending—being pelted by rocks—the behavior of the master and his squire. The former wants to go after the enemy, but

Don Quixote, when he saw them . . . in such a gallant squadron, with their arms raised ready to let fly a massive discharge of stones, reined in Rocinante and began to consider in what manner he could assail them with the least danger to his person. [P. 602]

And in that moment of reflection—so atypical of Don Quixote's usual unreflective conduct—Sancho comes up to him, now in his new role of counselor, and tells him, among other things:

"though they look like kings, princes . . . there's not one single knight errant."
"Now indeed," said Don Quixote, "you have hit the point that can and should turn me." [P. 602]

And he adds with a tenderness that is quite significant in this case too:

Since that is your resolve . . . good Sancho, wise Sancho, Christian Sancho, sincere Sancho, let us leave these phantoms alone. [P. 602]

These are all words that spring profusely when he feels he has been understood to the very depths of his being—which is the foundation of his game. But I think that among all those epithets, there is one in particular which holds the key here: "sincere Sancho." Why does he mention sincerity? Is it not possible, as some modern psychologists think, that it is one of those slips that our subconscious surreptitiously compels us to say or do—in spite of the inhibitions of our intellect and our consciousness? Could it not be that Don Quixote, knowing he is insincere when he looks for pretexts, is alluding to a sincerity incongruent with the words of Sancho, whose words evidently were not spoken to be judged in the light of that criterion?

And now we come to the adventure of the Knight of the Mirrors. But let us notice for once an incident in the tale into which we can put our own comment. I am referring to Don Quixote's thoughts on drama:

the ornaments of the drama should not be real, but only make-believe . . . like the drama itself. [P. 603]

Here we have a judgment much like another of his when he says: "a man who wants to play the part of a fool on stage must never be one."

What is important here is to see that Cervantes' idea of art is contained in that concept of the drama (along with the phrase already quoted about what is written down and what is omitted), to the point where it can be put into words: to paint reality—not with real elements, but with make-believe, fictional ones—which is what we find in the Knight of the Mirrors, a make-believe, fictional knight. But if we think at any length about it, what is Don Quixote himself? Could we find any clearer statement about what Don Quixote is doing? He is acting out a role. But we know that the only way to do a thing like this well, is "to go inside the character." Or, in other words, to play. In Spanish, the phrase is "*hacer un papel.*" But in French, for example, they say "*jouer le rol.*" And in English, an actor "plays a part." In the two latter cases, it is play. And children, who do not say anything, act better than anyone when they play.

Since all this might offend the pure ears of some Cervantista, I think the time has come for me to make a few clarifications. When I say that Don Quixote is playing, or when I claim that he is acting, I am not trying to suggest that he is a fake. His motivation is always the highest: with a pure soul. But to be able to assert and maintain this, there are times when outside events make him come to the point of acting. If we wish to recall Dostoevski's observation about *Don Quixote* being the most important book in Christian literature, but at the same time useless to live by, we might say that Don Quixote's motivation is always musical. And many times, if not always, it appears as "celestial music" [1]— and the "lyrics" to this music carry him to the point of reciting as well as acting. Aside from this, I think that my constant references to Myshkin or to Tom Sawyer and Huck will guard me from any such "blasphemy."

This is all greatly clarified by Sancho's words in his conversation with the Knight of the Mirrors' squire. When Sansón Carrasco's servant says that his master is "more roguish than crazy or valiant," Sancho says of his master:

Mine is not [roguish] like that. . . . On the contrary, he has a soul as simple as a pitcher: he could do no harm to anyone, but good to all, nor has he any malice in him: why, a child would convince him it is night at noonday, and it is on account of this simplicity that I love him as I love the cockles of my heart, and I can't invent a way of leaving him, no matter what piece of foolishness he does. [P. 613]

Let us remember that it has not been long since Sancho came upon those gold coins. So then: could Sancho's words about his master be used to define the relationship between Huck and Tom? Huck undoubtedly thinks Tom is "batty," but he also loves him as he loves the cockles of his heart—no matter what piece of "foolishness" he does. For those foolish things are the strongest link that could tie Sancho to Don Quixote, and Huck to Tom: magic, the game, which Sancho and Huck are not capable of inventing by themselves, but are able to follow with the ebullience of their souls.

[1] "música celestial": In Spanish, a conceit indicating that which is divine and useless at the same time. (Trans. note.)

This is the link, of course, and not the treasures—or the islands—which, for the squires, constitute nothing more, let us say, than the practical pretext that justifies them inwardly. That is why, in order to calm their sensible consciousness, they say and even believe that they are not following their guides for the game itself, but for the treasures. But this "sincere" Sancho has just let us see nothing less than the cockles of his heart. And to prove the point, notice that there is also a parallel—not mentioned by anyone, as far as I know—between Sancho's "abdication" as governor of the island and Huck's "sale" of his $6,000 for $1. As it will be remembered, at the end of *Tom Sawyer*, Tom and Huck find a treasure that brings them $6,000 apiece. The honorable and fatherly Judge Thatcher, to protect Huck from his father's greed, proposes to administer this very real fortune. Huck agrees. But Huck's father finds out about the existence of the treasure, and tries to get hold of it. Under these circumstances, Huck goes to the Judge:

"Why, my boy, you are all out of breath. Did you come for your interest?"

"No, sir . . . I don't want to spend it. I don't want it at all—nor the six thousand, nuther. I want you to take it; I want to give it to you—the six thousand and all." [P. 272]

And as the honest Judge becomes concerned, Huck begs him not to ask any questions that would make him tell a lie. Then the Judge finds the solution: to simulate a sale so that the boy's fortune can really remain intact. But the fact is that Huck was ready to give it all to him. The Judge concludes:

Oho-o! I think I see. You want to *sell* all your property to me—not give it. [P. 273]

He writes something on a piece of paper, and then says:

There; you see it says "for a consideration." That means I have bought it of you and paid you for it. Here's a dollar for you. Now you sign it. [P. 273]

And Huck signs and leaves. Is this any different from Sancho leaving his island? Let us leave the two "squires" here, and go to the Cervantian masters.

Now Sansón Carrasco deceitfully appears as the Knight of the Mirrors. But the Bachelor's deceit is everything Don Quixote could wish for: there are knights, duels because of noble motives, and so on. As a result, the two knights—"make-believe and fictional"—fight in singular combat and it happens that this time Don Quixote wins. He actually beats him. That is, this time he is not struck with sticks or stones. Only now there is that touch which is "also ridiculous"—which is something worse. What happens is that when Don Quixote removes the helmet from his defeated enemy, he sees . . . it is the face of Sansón Carrasco himself! Don Quixote cries out:

Come, Sancho, and behold what you have to see but not to believe; make haste, my son, and learn what magic can do; what wizards and enchanters are able to accomplish. [P. 624]

But now the knight is caught up in a moment of enthusiasm, and so, in spite of all the enchanters, he knows the steps he must take: he has conquered, and it was a fair contest. As a result, his historian notes:

He was extremely pleased, elated, and vainglorious at having won a victory over such a valiant knight. [P. 627]

We are now prepared to understand the great importance that Sansón Carrasco has for the novel. Due to him, for Don Quixote's point of view, every incident now has two versions, and one of them supports the game. While in the First Part the knight had to "make everything up"—as children say—making giants out of windmills (or Arabs out of Sunday-school children), now it is all true.

But let us go back to Don Quixote and his triumphant pride. The fact is that here too, in spite of the solemn assertion of his historian ("He was extremely pleased, elated and vainglorious"), Don Quixote is quite different inside. Let us look at what he himself—not his historian—says:

> It is all . . . an artifice and trick of the malignant magicians who persecute me and who, guessing that I was to be victorious in the conflict, settled that the vanquished knight should display the face of my friend the bachelor. [P. 630]

When the attribution of "friend" is invoked by Don Quixote we find a piece of perfect reasoning. How could there be friends interested in ruining us spiritually? (Even though friends may always be the ones who ruin us. But that is something else.)

What is important is that in the very same moment that Don Quixote shows such sureness of his reasoning powers, some of his own words let us see something more: the famous double thoughts of Myshkin. I believe that this consists of letting us see a Don Quixote who reasons so excellently but who, at the same time, shows an unspoken inner doubt about the identity of the Knight of the Mirrors. How are we shown this doubt—and, as a result, this double thought? In the very same proof that Don Quixote cites, when he is talking with Sancho, to try to convince him that "they changed" the Knight of the Mirrors.

And in proof, you know already, Sancho, through experience, which cannot lie or deceive, how easy it is for enchanters to change some countenances into others, making the beautiful ugly . . . [for] you saw with your own eyes the beauty [of] . . . Dulcinea in all its perfection . . . while I saw her [as] ugly. [P. 630]

Do we not see in this proof a subtle wink at his squire? Why does he say that Sancho's eyes cannot lie or deceive? In my opinion, it is because Don Quixote is aware. And because he is aware, he exerts pressure on the—hypocritical—conscience of his servant to restore the game: "because when all is said and done, I have been victorious over my enemy, no matter what shape he took." And Sancho can only agree to this, even when he does it enigmatically: "God knows the truth of it all."

And He knows it so well! Since Sancho knows it just as God does this time, he, Sancho, can only confirm the theory of enchantment. We have a supplementary proof of all this in the encounter with the knight of the green cloak. When Don Quixote notices the concern of his new companion, he utters those magnificent words:

I should not wonder if your worship were surprised at my appearance, which is . . . out of the ordinary. [P. 632]

Do madmen who think they are Napoleon talk like this? Why does he say this at precisely this moment, after the historian has finished telling us that he was so elated about his victory over the Knight of the Mirrors?

Because he is aware. Because now, even more than before, he is aware that the Knight of the Mirrors is the Bachelor, Sansón Carrasco, in disguise; because he knows that he, Don Quixote himself, left Toboso without wanting to see "Ducinea." And so, "I should not wonder . . ." Let us see at greater length a part of what Don Quixote says:

I have sought to revive the now extinct order of knight-errantry, and for many a day, stumbling here, falling there, flung down in one place and rising up in another, I have been accomplishing a great part of my design. [P. 632]

Up to here he tells us just one thing clearly: that he has been accomplishing a great part of his design. But he does not tell us with the same lucidity what his falling and rising has been. After this moment, however, Don Quixote not only rises, but he flies off on a tangent.

succoring widows, protecting maidens, and relieving wives, orphans and young children. [P. 632]

We cannot say that he is lying: there is some truth in the material deeds and much more in the spiritual ones, since Don Quixote has not only wanted to do such things, but he has done them—at least in a couple of specific cases: Andresillo, the galley slaves. But if we cannot say that he is lying, we can indeed maintain that he is exaggerating. Where were the widows, maidens, and the others? He knows that there have not been any—at least not yet—but he mixes things together a little to accentuate the game. And now all this is possible for him because of something he carries within himself: the knowledge of his victory over the Knight of the Mirrors, "no matter what shape he took," and because of something more, very much more, important for his game. Something he says without concealing it with false modesty:

and so, by my many valiant and Christian deeds I have been found worthy to appear in print in almost all, or at least most, of the nations of the earth. [P. 632]

But what are Tom Sawyer's "splendid days"—according to his historian?

Tom was a glittering hero once more—the pet of the old, envy of the young. His name even went into immortal print, for the village paper magnified him. [P. 169]

This, the knowledge that one is in print—which is one more unnoticed coincidence—is an important point not only for the characters, but for the authors of both books (if we call the two by Mark Twain only one). Really—and this has been noted in both cases—the fame of the books *Don Quixote* and *Tom Sawyer* was, to a great extent, the motivation for writing the Second Part of *Don Quixote,* just as it was for writing *Huckleberry Finn.*

Now let us look at the adventure of the lions. But since, in a way, this takes place for the benefit of the knight of the green cloak, let us notice that in his conversation with Don Quixote, the latter makes an important quasi-confession for the first time in the entire book:

There is much to be said . . . on this point of whether the stories of knights-errant are fictitious or not. [P. 633]

So we could say that this adventure of the lions involves two aspects. The one didactic in its lesson for the green-cloaked doubters of pure effort; and the other one essential, which shows us here an adventure par excellence. Don Quixote begins it with this incredible boast:

To this Don Quixote answered, smiling slightly: "Lion cubs to me? To me lion cubs? At such a time, too?" [P. 640]

At no other time, before or after, do we see Don Quixote involved in bragging. But, nevertheless, Cervantes not only makes him say these things, but also he has put in "smiling slightly" which in itself is material for a whole discourse. But he does all this after having noted, indirectly but very explicitly, the real and concrete danger of this adventure: the lions are "very large" and "now they are hungry." Why do we have that touch of bragging?

Let us leave the question on this point open for the moment, in order to see how Don Quixote's "descendants" face dangers that are described to us as real and concrete. Is there not a real danger when Tom Sawyer goes to the tavern where Injun Joe is sleeping? And in that light—in the boy's view of the fearful criminal—who is, in a sense, also "hungry now"—do we not see Don Quixote's childlike soul—within his game, yes, but really brave within that game? And furthermore, are we not aware of the danger that Prince Myshkin is running when he knows positively that Rogozhin—also "hungry"—is hiding on that sinister staircase, to kill him? And does not Myshkin, too, go bravely toward the danger? Shortly before the paragraphs that we are going to put down, the Prince remembers something he saw that morning in Rogozhin's hand: a knife with a horn handle:

He was just at the entrance of the gateway when he moved on abruptly after his momentary halt. And he suddenly saw in the half dark under the gateway . . . a man. . . . But he suddenly felt a complete and overwhelming conviction that he recognized the man and that it was certainly Rogozhin. . . . "Everything will be decided now," he repeated to himself with strange conviction. . . . On the first half-landing there was a hollow like a niche in the column, not more than a half a yard wide and nine inches deep. Yet there was room for a man to stand there. . . . Rogozhin's eyes flashed and a smile of fury contorted his face. His right hand was raised and something gleamed in it; Myshkin did not think of checking it. He only remembered that he thought he cried out, "Parfyon, I don't believe it!" [Pp. 266–267]

Now let us look at Don Quixote's behavior. Boldly and on foot, he awaits the lion; the animal does not want to come out and confines itself to turning its back on him. The knight orders the lionkeeper to prod it with a stick, and finally he emerges the victor in a real adventure. Notice carefully the way Cervantes tells it: it is an adventure and at the same time it is credible. So that it will not exceed the bounds of credibility, he has made the lion pay no attention to "childish bravado," for it turned around and "showed its hind parts" to Don Quixote. But it cannot be denied that Don Quixote has demonstrated what he had to, without ceasing to be the knight of a chivalresque novel—with adventures that are absurd and incredible.

Now let us summarize the three cases: When Tom decides to enter Injun Joe's "lair," the latter is asleep and drunk (i.e., "he showed his hind parts"), and so Tom has accepted the risk without perishing, but in a feasible and plausible way. As for Rogozhin, Myshkin's "hungry lion," he stands paralyzed before the Prince's epileptic attack—just at the very moment when the dagger is poised to strike. A logical and plausible solution, within the context of the entire novel. But the fact is that here too the beast "showed its hind parts" to the Prince. In all three cases, their respective authors—and each in a perfectly original way—wanted to place their characters in a situation with real danger, and have them face it courageously. But they also wanted a solution by which the protagonist is saved in a feasible and plausible way, and showing in each of the incidents three accounts of pure souls. I do not believe that this has been noticed either, but nonetheless it could not be more significant as far as the inner relationship of the three characters is concerned.

With regard to Cervantes, it is obvious that here he not only wants there to be a real adventure, but also a real victory. I mean to say, and quite seriously too, Cervantes is not poking fun here: he is asserting something, heroically asserting it, but in a human way and so "also ridiculous," as Dostoevski observed. As for Don Quixote, now that everything has become real, now that he has conquered very large and hungry lions, in a burst of enthusiasm he exclaims:

I am not bound to do more. Away with enchantments and God protect right [and] truth. [P. 644]

And in his enthusiast virtue—and in his candor—when all the terrified men come back and the lionkeeper stands as an official witness to the knight's valor, Don Quixote turns to Sancho:

What do you think of this, Sancho? . . . Are any enchantments able to prevail against true valor? The enchanters

may be able to rob me of good luck, but of courage they cannot. [P. 645]

As we know, these are words that have given rise to a great deal of worthy philosophical thought. Among other ideas, there is what Ortega calls "the critique of pure effort." But rather than philosophy, we have concrete novelesque material here: Don Quixote is bursting with happiness because of his triumph, and as a result, "away with enchantments," for these enchantments are his usual refuge from the nearly constant frustration that events persist in dealing to him. I think the reason could not be more evident: now that it is true, he does not need enchanters; he only needs them . . . at other times. In other words, Don Quixote is not crazy, "he knows." And if he knows and still acts the way he does, he is doing what children do: he is playing.

It is noteworthy that here Don Quixote is perfectly conscious of what he has done. As soon as he rejoins the green-cloaked knight, he says:

Nevertheless . . . I am not . . . mad. . . . But finer [it] is to see a knight-errant . . . in quest of perilous adventures. . . . [Let the other knights serve as they wish], but let the knight errant . . . encounter at every step the impossible. . . . So, it was strictly my right to attack these lions whom I attacked just now . . . [since] I knew it to be rash temerity. [P. 646]

Would not children really commit—and do they not, in fact, commit—a thousand acts of "rash temerity"?

Shifting now from lions to weddings, let us go to Camacho's. Speaking with Basilio about his wedding plans, Don Quixote unexpectedly says something that could well be called surprising:

I myself am not married, nor, so far, has it even come into
my mind to be so. [2] [P. 679]

And he says it like this, without a second thought.
And what about Dulcinea then? Will he go on looking
for her as if she were his mistress, as Sancho suggested
in El Toboso with a tone of moral recrimination? How
should we understand these words? Since Don Quixote's behavior leaves no room for doubt on that point,
there must be another answer. Don Quixote is not
thinking—nor has he ever thought—about marrying, in
spite of the fact that he always has on his lips the name
of a woman whom he says he idolizes—because he
knows: you can't, you're dead. Don Quixote plays at
being "in love," just as he plays at being "Hernán
Cortés." The author of the novel, however, does not
tell us that—among other things—clearly like this, but
gives us two historical versions, which are completely
contradictory. In this case there are more than two:
first, mention is made of Aldonza Lorenzo, and that he
had seen her a couple of times, and then the information—also historical—is added that "she had a good
hand at salting pork"; but later on Don Quixote says
that he has never seen her, and "he was enamoured
only by hearsay" and now, to finish it off, he declares
simply that he has never thought about marrying. Is all
this not more than enough to make us understand? I
will return to this again when I talk about the loves of
Don Quixote.

[2] I am reproducing here Rodríguez Marín's note on this point, because I consider it significant. He says: "It would only befit a madman
to have this changeableness. How could a man as much in love as
Don Quixote—who took the barber's prophecy of 'the soft yoke of
matrimony' with good will—not think about marriage?" Miguel de
Cervantes, *El ingenioso hidalgo Don Quijote de la Mancha*, Edición
crítica por F. Rodríguez Marín, 6 vols. (Madrid: Ed. Imprenta de la
'Revista de archivas, bibliotecas y museos', 1916), IV, 444.

In the following chapters we are told about the events in the Cave of Montesinos. And on this point, since I find Menéndez Pidal's analysis of this adventure absolutely superb, I can only refer the reader to his writings. To give some idea about that theory, let us recall a few lines:

This is the only time that Don Quixote stands alone in the world of "improbability" without the adverse corrective. The mechanics of the entire novel, fantasy-reality, are suspended on this occasion only. [II, 208]

And then, comparing Don Quixote with Ajax, he concludes:

The hero of Salamis kills himself when he feels like a laughingstock before the reality that he sees, he kills himself out of self-shame; the Manchegan hero dies from sadness at life, when he discovers that reality is inferior to him. [II, 208–209]

In the first place I would say that nobody dies from "sadness at life," but from illnesses, such as Don Quixote has, according to Cervantes:

he was stricken down by a violent fever that confined him to his bed for six days. [P. 1044]

Furthermore, in Don Quixote's case the opposite may be happening: when he realizes that he is dying he becomes sad, with the great sadness of knowing that games are worthless when confronted by death. I will try to show this in the chapter entitled *The Moment of Truth*. For the moment let us remember that among the things Don Quixote "saw" in the cave, one of them is an enchanted Dulcinea. But Sancho "thought he would die with laughter" over that, since he knew the truth about Dulcinea's enchantment. As a result, he reproaches his master for "blabbering the greatest balderdash that ever was known." And the strange fact is that Don Quixote does not get angry when he sees he is being treated like a madman, and by his own squire, at that. And he gently answers: "I know you Sancho, so I pay no heed to your words," which is a great deal to concede. But there is still more, as we shall see in the Adventure of Clavileño. Without waiting for that time, however, we can still come to some conclusion. Since the author of this story, and Menéndez Pidal too (although not from the same point of view, of course), assure us that the knight is not lying, which I agree with completely, the solution that arises is one, and only one. Don Quixote is telling something—as we used to do when we were children—that we call true and yet that never happened. In other words, the magic that Menéndez Pidal sees—which is real—that kind of a dream, is called playing, in the world of children. I think that is why we have the scruples of the author, who writes about this adventure:

whose impossibility and immensity has caused this adventure to be considered apocryphal. [P. 686]

And then:

all the adventures until now have been feasible and plausible, but this one of the cave I can find no way of accepting it as true. [P. 696]

We are dealing with a descent into a world of real magic. That is, we cannot accept it with the same criterion we use for the rest of the book. And since (as

Menéndez Pidal surmises) Cervantes does not want to renounce it, this has to be taken as a dream. Or, in any case, something that Don Quixote fully realizes has a complete nonreality. In other words—and the affair with Clavileño proves it—here Don Quixote knows. But he "knows" in another way. When he asserts that an inn is a castle, he knows the truth: that is why he does not doubt. And also that is why he has doubts now.

The matter of Maese Pedro's puppet show is its own commentary. When Maese Pedro—Ginés de Pasamonte, the galley slave freed by Don Quixote—sees Don Quixote, he decides to use the knight's presence at the inn for the success of his "prophetic ape." The ape's performance actually leaves them all mystified. That is, the most plausible and roguish reality serves as a material basis for the most delicate game. Aside from this, what happens in the puppet show does not amount to much. We have an abducted woman, powerful and wicked men, good men who are oppressed, and so, material for Christian charity to work on. Don Quixote, filled with enthusiast virtue, draws his sword, and swings it with both hands "upon the puppet Moors." Does this need any clarification? Do we all not have memories of similar "victories"?

Even though it is in passing, let us listen to a transcendental braying. And supposing that everyone recalls "hearing" it, let us see what the historian says about Don Quixote:

When a valiant man flees, it is obvious that there is foul play. . . . This truth was verified in Don Quixote, who, giving way to the fury of the villagers . . . took to his heels . . . without thinking of Sancho or of the peril he was in. [P. 727]

A counterpoint to the adventure with the lions, Don Quixote's flight in this braying adventure gives rise to a rift between the master and his servant. Sancho will not forgive him:

But I can't help telling how knights-errant take to their heels and leave their good squire . . . [in] the hands of their enemies. [P. 728]

Despite everything, these words have no answers. For this reason, Don Quixote has a bad conscience, as his words show ("Retreat is not flight")—which are so contrary to his deliberate "rash temerity" with the lions. Concerning all this—and this is what is important here—they begin to figure out how much Sancho should be paid for his services. And Sancho says that he has been serving his master "twenty years, and three days more or less."

Don Quixote gave himself a great slap on the forehead and began to laugh heartily, saying: "Why, I scarcely traveled two months in the Sierra Morena or in all the course of our sallies; yet, how can you say, Sancho, that it is twenty years?" [P. 730]

Is it really not strange that a knight who is so systematic about taking inns for castles, prostitutes for maidens, and so forth, should have such a good memory for the actual place—Sierra Morena—and the actual time —two months? But there is still something more. Don Quixote, partly out of generosity, and partly to placate his bad conscience, consents to all of Sancho's calculations. The latter has already been holding all his master's money. But the two still have to settle their spiritual account. And now we see that the initiative changes hands. If the reproaches were on Sancho's lips

before, now it is Don Quixote who passes to the offensive. And it is such an offensive that Sancho cannot
stand up to it at all. It consists of reproaches of ingrati-
tude combined with new promises:

O ill-requited bread! . . . O man more beast than human!
Now, when I was intending to set you up in state, and in
such a state that they would call you lord despite your
wife, now do you leave me? [P. 731]

And by that path of mischievous goodness—of mischief itself, completely childlike—Don Quixote gets
what he wants—to subdue Sancho—no matter how
much he or his historian keep quiet about it:

Sancho looked fixedly at Don Quixote while he was uttering
these reproaches, and he was so stricken with remorse that
the tears came into his eyes, and in a weak and doleful
voice he cried: "Master, I confess that all I need to be a
complete ass is the tail." [P. 731]

That excellent reconciliation scene, so moving because of the master's subtlety as well as the squire's
tender simplicity, is comparable to only one thing: the
quarrels of children. It has all been resolved—without
hard feelings—and each one goes back to his place in
the game. And immediately we see that this same
knight, who knew how to keep track of time so well,
has barely gotten into the "enchanted boat" when he
declares:

But we must already have emerged and traveled at least
two thousand miles, or more. If I had only an astrolobe
here with which I could take the height of the pole . . .
though either I know little or we have passed, or shall soon
pass, the equinoctial line. [P. 734]

Quixotic, high-sounding words, used at a moment of enthusiasm, and their use reestablishes the equilibrium. But this does not happen without Sancho translating his master's scientific vocabulary ("computation of Ptolemy, the best cosmographer") to a more homely language: "gaffer with his whorish amputation or I know not what."

With the Duke and Duchess

The historian begins the whole episode of the castle with a significant terseness: "Of what befell Don Quixote with a fair huntress." In a moment we will see why. But right now let us examine the lady's description:

The lady herself was clad in green of so rich and gorgeous texture that comeliness seemed to be personified in her. On her left hand she bore a hawk, a token by which Don Quixote knew that she must be some great lady and the mistress of all those hunters, which was true. [Pp. 739–740]

Notice the care that the historian takes to tell us that now it is true—in a certain sense. Also notice that as soon as Don Quixote sees her, he bursts out, "Run, Sancho, my son," but adds:

Mind, Sancho, how you speak, and be careful not to intrude any of your proverbs into the message. [P. 740]

This is a precaution in the character which agrees exactly with that of the historian when he tells us that now it is true—a half-truth, of course, like "The bubbles we pursue on earth,/The shapes we chase . . ."[3]

---

[3] "las cosas tras que andamos y corremos": Henry Wadsworth Longfellow's translation of the poem by Jorge Manrique, *Coplas por la muerte de su padre.* (Trans. note.)

Sancho delivers his message very well, and as a result we learn that she is "a beautiful lady of rank" who has "heard a great deal" about Don Quixote and who confirms the existence of the History. That is, on these pages a world opens up for the knight which is much more marvelous because it fully coincides, in a certain sense, with his own. Now we are not dealing with prostitutes or inns that must be made into maidens and castles respectively. Moreover, whatever happens, happens in a feasible and plausible way. So Don Quixote has an abundance of reasons for believing that everything is happening according to the rules: his books. And thanks to Cervantes, everything is this way, and yet, at the same time it is not this way. That is why, when Sancho says what he does:

Don Quixote preened himself in his saddle, set his feet taut in the stirrups, fixed his visor, dug his spurs into Rocinante, and with easy bearing advanced to kiss the hands of the duchess. [P. 741]

"Preened himself" is worthy of an entire psychological treatise. He "preens" himself precisely because now he feels that the game is true. But because of this, we should notice something that we could well call incredible and sensational, but that nonetheless is no more than a slight omission. Don Quixote greets the Duke, and turning to the Duchess, he adds:

your worthy consort, worthy mistress of beauty and universal princess of courtesy. [P. 742]

That the "omission" is not merely carelessness on the part of the historian is indirectly proved when the Duke reminds Don Quixote that where Dulcinea is, "it is not right that other beauties should be praised."

Why is it that now, at precisely this moment, when everything seems to fit Don Quixote's inner world, he "omits" mention of Dulcinea's name? Let us find out: if Cervantes has the knight make this omission—and the fact is that he, Cervantes, is so conscious of it that he has the Duke remind Don Quixote—how should we interpret that "eloquent silence" of the knight? I think the answer is obvious: because Don Quixote knows. And because he knows what happened in El Toboso (he did not want to see Dulcinea), at this time when there actually is a beautiful woman, "he forgets" to mention Dulcinea because now it is not necessary. Or, rather, it would not have been necessary. But since they remind him, from this point on he will always exalt Dulcinea—but only in a certain way. We will look at this again later.

Let us continue, and we will see some incredible things. The Duke orders his servants to treat Don Quixote like a real knight—in a feasible and plausible way, so that everything will seem true, even though it is not. And before such magnificence, we are told:

All this astonished Don Quixote, and for the first time he felt thoroughly convinced that he was a knight-errant in fact and not in imagination, for he saw himself treated in the same way as he had read that such knights were treated. [P. 745]

So for once, as if in passing, the historian tells us everything: before now Don Quixote had never believed he was a knight-errant in fact, but only in imagination. But is this very thing not what we clearly and simply call playing? Could it be stated more plainly that, until now at least, Don Quixote has been playing the part of a knight, just as he was playing at being in love? And

does not the significance of that omission of Don Quixote's, when he introduces himself to the Duke and
Duchess, become clear?

Let us go on. After the introduction of the petty ecclesiastic—"one of those who would measure the greatness of grandees by their own narrowness of mind"—
we enter the dining room. There we have the courteous
formalities about who will sit at the head of the table,
and Sancho interrupts these formalities to tell a story:

**No sooner had Sancho said this than Don Quixote trem-
bled, for he was sure that his squire was about to deliver
himself of some piece of tomfoolery. [P. 749]**

Why that guardedness of Don Quixote? What makes
him tremble for Sancho? Ordinarily, does he not get
along very well with him? But the fact is that Don
Quixote is aware, and because he is, he knows that Sancho is not aware. There are things, certain things in the
game the knight and his squire bring with them, which
are delicate and subtle. And when examined closely,
those things sometimes require answers that are hardly
satisfactory to minds not well versed in matters of enchantment. In such cases (all the time, but never when
they are in society) when Sancho touches on one of
those "impossible" points, all that is necessary is for
Don Quixote—or Tom Sawyer—to give a slight touch
on the rudder to get back in the right direction: the
"We have had enough of this" of Don Quixote or the
"numskull" of Tom. And everything is in order. But we
should ask ourselves: what would have happened, for
example, if the conversation about the Arabs and the
elephants had occurred in public? We do not know, of
course, but I do believe we can guess that Tom would

have been on pins and needles too, very much afraid
that Huck might say some "piece of tomfoolery." Whatever the case, so that it can be seen this is not mere
speculation on my part, let us look at a particular instance of Tom's reticence to show himself in public with
his close friend (but one who is a close friend only
when they are alone). Both boys have heard Injun Joe
talking about the mysterious "number 2." Tom comes
to the conclusion:

> "Lemme think a minute. Here—it's the number of a
> room—in a tavern, you know!"
> "Oh, that's the trick! They ain't only two taverns. We
> can find out quick."
> "You stay here, Huck, till I come."
> Tom was off at once. He did not care to have Huck's
> company in public places. [Pp. 189–190]

Getting back to our story: Of the whole argument between Don Quixote and the ecclesiastic, which reaches
the point of the knight being called "Don Idiot," I will
give only the knight's last sentences:

> If knights . . . considered me an idiot, I should consider
> it as an irreparable affront. . . . Some choose the broad
> road of proud ambition, some that of mean and servile
> flattery . . . and a small number that of true religion; but
> I, influenced by my star, follow the narrow path of knight-
> errantry. [P. 754]

Notice that here too, just as when the Curate of his
village reproached him for having freed the galley
slaves, here too I say, Don Quixote places "true religion" above any ecclesiastic. I do not know how to emphasize enough the importance of those words. Because
if the critical aspect so well studied about Cervantes'

thought is in them, the assertion of his Christianity, or if you prefer, of his Christian radicalism—of a truly-beautiful soul—seems more significant to me.

Without going into detail about it now, let us examine the burst of enthusiasm that these words precipitate in Sancho. ("By God, that's great. Say no more . . . for there's no more . . . to be said.") Because when the ecclesiastic also faces Sancho to ask him if he is the Sancho Panza of the history, Sancho now affirms it, and sides completely with his master, and as a "consequence," the Duke—a real Duke!—gives him the governorship of an island, "an odd one of mine." So now the world of marvels is not for Don Quixote alone, but also for Huck Finn with the treasure found in the cave —I mean for Sancho with the governorship of his "real" island.

Let us look at another point. After the washing of beards, the Duchess brings out in the open the Dulcinea question. First she asks Don Quixote to describe her. And to answer her, the knight immediately begins to "recite" his role as a love-sick swain: "If I could tear out my heart and lay it . . . before your highness' eyes . . ." But the Duchess insists, referring to the History, from which she gathers:

that your worship has never seen Lady Dulcinea, and that this lady does not exist on earth but as a fantastical mistress whom your worship has begotten and brought forth in your mind. [P. 760]

When faced with this, if we had to judge by appearances, would it not be the moment for Don Quixote to explode, asserting that there is a Dulcinea? Is everything not the way it is in the books now? Is everything not true? If Don Quixote were a madman, would this,

more than ever, not be the time to affirm his Dulcinea,
whose charms he has extolled with such eloquence—
paragraphically—a moment before? And nonetheless,
Don Quixote evasively answers:

On that point there is much to say. . . . God knows whether
Dulcinea exists on earth or not, or whether she is fantastical
or not. These are not matters where verification can be
carried out to the full. [P. 760]

What more could we ask for? One of the greatest ad-
mirers of Cervantes, Flaubert, when questioned about
Madame Bovary, gave his famous answer: "madame
Bovary, c'est moi." Could we say that he is lying? And
on the other hand, could we say that it is the truth?
Don Quixote cannot be more explicit, nor does he want
to be: Dulcinea *is* Don Quixote.

Then, throughout this entire section with the Duke
and Duchess, there follow the diverse counterfeit adventures to make fun of Don Quixote. And he "falls for
them," of course. But when we say that he falls for
them, have we said everything?

When the Doleful Duenna is introduced, after the
fraudulent allusion of the Duke ("Virtue cannot be ob-
scured"), at first it seems that Don Quixote really
"bites" when he calls to mind the "blessed man of religion":

I wish, sir duke . . . that blessed man of religion were here
. . . that he might see with his own eyes whether such
knights are needed in the world. [P. 795]

but then he adds:

in desperate cases and appalling disasters [the destitute] do
not go to seek their remedy in the houses of scholars, nor

in those of village sacristans, nor from the knight who has never ventured beyond the boundaries of his town. [P. 795]

At whom are these words pointed? Cervantes keeps quiet, of course. But could we not say that we are being confronted with one of those double thoughts that so mortified Myshkin? Do we not see that these words could really be applied very well to the Duke himself? If Don Quixote were not a pure soul, he would have expressed it in a more decisive way, for he did not lack the courage to do it. But being the way he is, a pure soul, it is he who feels the shame the Duke should have felt for his own malice. Like Myshkin, Don Quixote also has that sharp sense of perception that the Prince shows at different times.

On this occasion, Don Quixote's words do not seem to be dictated by something clear, but by something quite obscure: his subconscious, and the famous double thoughts. Because Don Quixote has such nobility of spirit, he does not even dare think what the Duke in fact dares to do: to mock, to jeer. But thanks to that childlike state of Don Quixote, the mockery, the jeering itself supports Don Quixote's difficult game. But not without his having understood—as the episode of Clavileño proves later—what is really happening around him.

So let us examine the adventure of Clavileño. As it will be recalled, the most striking part at first is Sancho's fear, which Don Quixote comments on with somewhat ambiguous words:

Since that . . . adventure of the fulling mills . . . I have never seen Sancho in such fear as now, and if I were as superstitious as some are, his pusillanimity would cause me . . . heartthrobbing. [P. 814]

In the first place, Don Quixote makes an allusion to the adventure of the fulling mills, which he knows was a fiasco. Why does he call it to mind now? And, furthermore, although never admitting that he had been afraid in the past, he now alludes to "heartthrobbing." Throbbing from fear? We shall leave the question open for the moment. But let us look at his behavior the moment he mounts the horse, and at what he says to Sancho:

Blindfold yourself, Sancho, and mount, Sancho! For he who sends for us from such distant lands *will not deceive us*, seeing the scant glory he would gain from *defrauding one who trusts him*. But even supposing that everything should turn *contrary to my expectation*, no *malice* can obscure the glory of our having attempted this enterprise. [P. 815]

We will observe that in so few lines, words accumulate—underlined by me—which do not imply fear, but mistrust. But there is even more. He took out a handkerchief for the Doleful Duenna to cover his eyes, but as soon as it was done, he took the blindfold off again and said:

If I remember rightly, I have read in Virgil of the Trojan Palladium, which was the wooden horse that the Greeks presented to the Goddess Pallas and which was pregnant with armed knights who afterward wrought the total destruction of Troy. So, first it would be well to see what Clavileño carries in his stomach. [P. 815]

I do not think it could be stated better—and so implicitly—that Don Quixote was mistrustful, suspecting more malice: which is just what happens. So it is clear from this point on, although within a whole process of double thoughts that had been established before, possibly since the washing of beards, he knows what to expect from the Duke and Duchess. But it so happens—and here I am trying to tie the loose ends together—that in this same chapter, when Sancho tells him "what he saw in the sky," Don Quixote confidentially says to his squire:

if you want me to believe what you saw in the sky, I wish you to accept my account of what I saw in the Cave of Montesinos. [P. 821]

With this he alludes to the incredible, down to the point of striking a bargain—give and take. Why does this happen here, rather than anywhere else? In my opinion, I have no doubt that it is because Don Quixote has now come to understand and knows what kind of a castle he is in: an enchanted one, yes, but not with the same kind of enchantment he gave to the inns. I will attempt to prove this with the case of the Doleful Duenna. As it will be remembered, this particular Doleful Duenna turns out to be the Duke's steward. Since Sancho recognizes him, and after many oaths and exclamations, shows his master the real truth of the situation, Don Quixote replies:

There is no reason why the devil should carry you off, Sancho . . . for the Doleful One's face is just like the steward's; yet for all that, the steward is not the Doleful One, for if this were so, it would imply too great a contradiction. However, this is not the time for going into all that, as it would involve us in an endless labyrinth. [Pp. 834–835]

Apparently we are being confronted with a typical case: Don Quixote disposes of the difficulty with one stroke: you are a numskull. But I think there is something else within the knight, since he knows about the endless labyrinths that these investigations would involve. For, as if by chance, in this same chapter and almost immediately after the above passages, the knight undergoes one of those twinges of melancholy which from now on he will have more and more frequently. I am referring to the phrase that has been commented on so much:

As soon as Sancho had departed [to be governor] Don Quixote felt an acute sense of loneliness, and had it been in his power to cancel the commission and deprive Sancho of his government, he would have done it. [P. 835]

Let us look at this a little more closely. It so happens that the Duchess herself notices what is happening to him, and asks him if his sadness is due to Sancho's departure. But Don Quixote, although he does not deny that "he misses Sancho," adds:

but that is not the principal cause of my apparent sadness. I must decline all of your grace's kind offers except the goodwill with which they are tendered. [P. 836]

If we look closely at all this, I think that we can really say that necessity joins desire here. He misses Sancho, of course. But for what reason does he miss him? To play. Don Quixote knows very well that Sancho is the only one who plays well, who plays clean— like Huck Finn. But besides that absence of the moment, it is even more painful because Don Quixote knows that something is happening which is not very kosher: the Doleful One, Clavileño, and other things.

If he were really a simple madman, would he not have ended up losing his wits completely in that enchanted castle with the offerings of the Duke and Duchess, and all the rest? But Cervantes' smile comes in to let us understand: at this moment, when everything seems to fit together, now is when Don Quixote feels—even though it is still vaguely—the mockery that surrounds him, the sideshow they are making of him, and as a result he feels sad; he feels his loneliness. Is it not significant, almost too significant to mention, that it is here, at this precise moment, when the adventure of Altisidora begins to take shape? For that reason it deserves a separate chapter. But for what we are observing now, it is important to notice part of what Don Quixote says in his letter to Sancho, the Governor.

After asking his squire if there was anything in the resemblance of the steward to La Trifaldi (so that we can see he was still bothered by the question), as if he does not care for this affair, he adds:

particularly as I intend soon to leave this idle life I am living at present, for I was not born for it. [P. 895]

And after this declaration, which seems like both a statement of principle and a beginning but is really an end, he adds in closing:

A certain matter has arisen that I believe will involve me in disgrace with the Duke and Duchess. But though it concerns me, it does not affect my decision at all, for after all, when it comes to the point, I must comply with my profession rather than with their pleasure, for as the saying goes, *Amicus Plato, sed magis amica veritas.* I say this in Latin, for I suppose that since you have become a governor you have learned it. [Pp. 895–896]

With all this, Don Quixote shows two things: first, that he is fed up with the Duke and Duchess—putting it

plainly; and second, dazzled by the possibility of re-
newing the game merely by talking with his squire and
companion, he feels himself understood so deeply that
he returns to the enchanted type of reasoning: since
you are a governor, you must know Latin.

As for the first point, we should ask: Why is Don
Quixote fed up with the Duke and Duchess? Is it only
because he is idle? Does he really not remember the
first day he arrived at the castle—when, for the first
time, he "believed" he was a knight errant in fact and
not in imagination? What has happened then? I do not
believe it could be stated any more clearly, either, that
now Don Quixote is aware. And for that reason, he can
hardly wait to leave. But an incident caused by a
stupid duenna—Doña Rodríguez, and the affront
against her daughter—will keep him there. We would
expect the knight to throw himself enthusiastically into
the adventure. Nevertheless we see a reticent, realistic
Don Quixote here who, referring to the daughter, says:

it would have been wiser of her not to have put such easy
trust in a lover's promises, for most of them are quick to
promise but mighty slow to perform. [P. 900]

At this precise moment, when there is a real lady in
distress to protect, Don Quixote begins to make excuses
and preach sermons. Is this behavior not strange? In
my opinion, it can only be explained by the clear mistrust he has of the castle. But in spite of it all—and this
is essential—when between the sword of a real affront
and the wall of his knightly principles, Don Quixote
does not hesitate. As a pure soul, he goes to the duel,
and puts his life at stake, even for something in which
—as a knight—he does not believe. Could there be a
higher heroism?

As a commentary on this whole matter of the Duke and Duchess, we see that when Don Quixote abandons the castle and finds himself in the country with Sancho again, he intones what we could very well call a hymn to liberty:

Liberty, Sancho, my friend, is one of the most precious gifts that Heaven has bestowed on mankind. . . . For liberty, as well as for honor, man ought to risk even his life, and he should reckon captivity the greatest evil life can bring. [P. 935]

A hymn, all of it, and seemingly in paragraphs. But I believe it recovers all its sentiment when, with real double thoughts, it refers to "captivity" even though it seems incongruent with their situation. Could Don Quixote tell us with any more clarity what he thinks about the castle and its owners?

Now he is back in the countryside again, with Sancho, in the open fields. Long live liberty!

5

The Loves of
Don Quixote

On previous pages we have seen the character of
Don Quixote, "totally in love" with Dulcinea: knights
are in love; I am a knight; *ergo* I am in love. That is,
Dulcinea is part of the game. I think that the complex,
contradictory versions are sufficient to show this: Dulcinea is Aldonza Lorenzo; then, Don Quixote had seen
her only two or three times; later he has never seen
her; on still another occasion he says he has not married nor has he ever thought of doing such a thing; finally, when the Duchess asks him if he might not have
begotten her in his mind, and is she not a fantastical
mistress, Don Quixote enigmatically answers: "God
knows whether she is fantastical or not."

Let us go on, then, to examine the loves of Don Quixote. But before doing this, I think it is necessary to es-
tablish how all this has been viewed. Mrs. Turkevich,

in her reference to Bem, tells us, when summarizing his thesis:

> Even his [Chatski's] attitude towards women, to which Bem points, has a texture different from Myshkin's. It is passionate, blinding him to actual circumstances, whereas that of Myshkin, Don Quixote, and the Poor Knight is chaste, pure—sexless. [P. 124]

And then, expressing her own opinion, she says:

> Myshkin loves Nastasya Filipovna and Aglaya fervently, but not passionately. Like Don Quixote, he is ignorant of woman, except as aspects of his ideal. Physical love would have been just as great a betrayal of his ideal as it would have been in the case of Don Quixote. [P. 129]

Evidently chastity, the simple chastity of a pure soul, has not seemed like a sufficient explanation. But in my judgment, this is what best explains Don Quixote as well as Myshkin to us: their quality of childlike souls. Because being a beautiful soul does not in any way imply that one stops belonging to the human race and becomes an angel, or a creature without sex—to be precise.

Now let us remember the verb Cervantes used to tell us what the knight did when he saw "a fair huntress": "he preened himself." So then I would say that this is what Don Quixote does as soon as there is a beautiful woman in sight: he preens himself. But he does this on two occasions in particular: before the innkeeper's daughter in the First Part, and with Altisidora in the Second. Now notice that in Myshkin's case, he is in love with Aglaia, but he also feels a certain something for Nastasya Filippovna. No matter how many excuses one makes, the fact still remains in the text: Myshkin,

in love with Aglaia, is also attracted to Nastasya Filippovna.

The Daughter

Now let us go to the inn in the First Part. Don Quixote arrives there, bruised and battered. Immediately
three women enter the scene: the innkeeper's wife, "by
nature kindhearted"; her daughter, "young, a very good
looking lass"; and Maritornes, the Asturian, "flat pated."
We are told that Maritornes and the Daughter (that is
what we will call her, for the name of that "very good
looking" young lady is not preserved) healed the knight
"as well as they could." But we are also told that when
Sancho reveals who they are: a knight-errant and his
squire, Don Quixote, "as best he could" sat up in the
bed, and "taking the landlady by the hand," he recited,
let us say, one of his paragraphs: "Believe me beautiful
lady, you may call yourself fortunate in having har-
bored," and so on, a tirade the last part of which interests us:

Would to heaven that love had not enthralled me and sub-
jected me to its laws and to the eyes of the beautiful in-
grate whose name I whisper to myself, else would the eyes
of this beauteous damsel here bereave me of my freedom.
[P. 155]

Let us pay close attention: Don Quixote is laid out,
but this does not stop him from preening himself.
Beaten and all, we see that he has scrutinized very
closely the girl's very good looking appearance. But
that is not everything. Beaten and all, Don Quixote
draws on all the strength he can muster to sit up in bed

and deliver, with great ease, a real declaration of love.
Of course, it all seems to be subject to an "if": if I
were not in love. But that does not make the declaration any less explosive. That is why the three women:

although they didn't understand the words, they realized
that they were compliments and offers of service . . .
thanking him in their rough pothouse phrases for his offers.
[P. 155]

The tale is momentarily interrupted here without the
author telling us clearly what Don Quixote is thinking.
But without having to make a hypothesis, we still see it
perfectly. As it will be remembered, Maritornes goes
looking for the carrier. And the historian makes a preparatory comment:

All the inn was sunk in silence, and there was no other
light but that of a lantern that hung in the middle of the
gateway. [P. 156]

In that "wonderful stillness," Don Quixote begins
thinking about his books. And the author—as always—
tells us that the character is mad. All this:

brought to his imagination one of the strangest follies. . . .
He fancied that he was now in a famous castle . . . and
that the landlord's daughter . . . captivated by his gallant
presence, had fallen in love with him and had promised to
lie with him that night for a good space of time without
her parents being any the wiser. . . . He began to feel
anxious as he reflected on the perils that his honor would
suffer, but he resolved in his heart not to be guilty of the
least infidelity to his lady, Dulcinea of El Toboso. [P. 157]

Does one have to be Freud to interpret all this as a
subconscious realization of desires in which even that

type of vow of chastity becomes fully significant as a
defense mechanism? Dulcinea becomes a kind of cen-
soring screen for what is forbidden. And if this first
part—this verbal declaration—seems of little import, it
will immediately become something different: no less
chaste, of course, but much more significant as we shall
see in the continuation of the scene. But now I think
that we can set down something definite: Don Quixote
is playing at being in love with Dulcinea; but, apart
from the game, Don Quixote is a man. And even
though he has a pure soul, that does not stop him from
being a man—a male; nor, as a result, does he stop
feeling the feminine attraction, no matter how censored
it may appear. But the text proves it to us better than
my words do:

**While he lay thinking of these follies, the hour came . . .
when the Asturian wench . . . entered the room . . .
scarcely had she reached the door when Don Quixote
heard her, and sitting up in his bed, despite the plasters
. . . pulling her toward him (not a word did she dare to
utter), made her sit down on the bed. Then he felt her
shift, and though it was of sackcloth, he thought it was
made of the finest and most delicate lawn, [etc.] [P. 157]**

That is, Don Quixote has gone into action. And now
begins the duel between the external and internal reality of Don Quixote: sackcloth-lawn; horsehair-threads
of gold from Arabia. But all this, to end with giving,
"in a low, tender voice," a whole new declaration of
love—although he finishes by invoking his beating and
his fidelity to Dulcinea—fifty-fifty?—as an excuse:

**Had this obstacle not intervened, I should not be so doltish
a knight as to let slip the happy opportunity thy great
bounty has bestowed upon me. [P. 158]**

I think that we should ask ourselves: to what point is Don Quixote telling the truth, and where does he not tell it? When he recognizes Maritornes—although he denies it—and thinking as he does about the Daughter, to what point is his declamation simply a compensation for his disillusionment? Let us leave these questions open for the moment and listen to the conversation that Don Quixote and Sancho finally hold about the events that have just happened. And here the knight, after many scrupulous reservations about "refusing to take away the good name of anyone," says the following:

Briefly [the adventure] was as follows: A little while ago I was visited by the daughter of the lord of this castle, who is the most talented and beautiful damsel to be found over a great part of the earth. What could I not tell you of the charm of her person? . . . What of those other hidden things I shall let pass untouched and unspoken, to keep the faith I owe to my lady, Dulcinea of El Toboso? [P. 161]

Now it is not I who am speaking, but Don Quixote himself. And if his first question can still be considered a result of the magic I have been talking about, and we can accept the possibility that Don Quixote really does not recognize Maritornes, it is not possible to say the same about his second question. What "hidden things" will Don Quixote "let pass untouched and unspoken"? He is lying. The knight is actually lying. But he is lying like a small boy who pretends he is a man. And that is the real significance of his lie: while he was with Maritornes-Daughter, he conducted himself like a chaste man, but when he is with Sancho—his friend—he has to brag and talk about "hidden things."

If we were to consider the matter of the Daughter as incidental to Cervantes' intentions, the adventure could have ended there. But is that the case? Not at all. The subject comes up again, not only in the knight's thoughts, but with the Daughter herself involved. Words are said about her, for example, that even today, when seen in a certain light, would not lose their significance for many. When Sancho says he also feels bruised from "the sudden fright I took on seeing my master fall," the Daughter remarks:

I myself have often dreamed that I was falling from some high tower without ever coming to the ground. [P. 154]

This is a dream that I think is still characteristic. It could be a minor point, if there were not other facts. But they do exist. After all the adventures in the castle-inn, and after the very different effects that the balsam of Fierabrás has on the master and on his servant, when Don Quixote mounts his horse to leave, we read:

All the people that were staying in the inn, over twenty in number, stood staring at him. The innkeeper's daughter was also staring at him, and Don Quixote kept gazing at her fixedly, and from time to time he breathed forth so doleful a sigh that it seemed he had plucked it from the bottom of his heart. All, however, or at least those who had seen him plastered the night before, thought that the sighs must have been caused by the pain in his ribs. [P. 165]

We are not told more here—but what we have been told is a great deal. What does the girl who has weird dreams think, when she sees a weird man—and so very weird!—that from the very first minute she does not take her eyes off him? We do not know. Probably, she does not exactly know either. But we can be sure of one thing: she knows the truth about the meaning of those deep sighs of Don Quixote.

Now everything seems to have come to an end. The story of the Daughter, like the Guadiana River, goes underground and is forgotten; but, like the river, it comes to the surface again. Is it not odd that a character to whom Cervantes does not even give a name will come back to flourish at the story's surface? Let us see how she reappears. When Don Quixote and Sancho let themselves be taken back to the inn, the Curate shortly afterward makes his inquiry into novels of chivalry. And when he speaks to the Daughter, she answers:

Ah, Father . . . I don't know. I also listen to them; and though I don't understand, I take pleasure in hearing them. But I don't like the blows that delight my father; only the lamentations that the knights make when they are away from their ladies sometimes make me weep, so much pity do I feel for them. [P. 321]

At that point the discreet Dorotea asks her if she would mend their sorrows out of compassion, and the Daughter declares:

I do not know what I would do. . . . I only know that some of those ladies are so cruel that their knights call them tigresses and lionesses . . . . But Lord save us! What kind of people are they? Can they be so heartless and unfeeling that they prefer to let an honorable man die or go mad . . . ? If they pretend to be honest women, why don't they marry them, seeing that they long for nothing else? [P. 321]

These are words that give us the sentimental makeup of the girl—fond of novels and such—which helps us understand the well-known look when she says goodbye to Don Quixote. The incident appears again in the adventure of the wineskins, when the landlady bawls about the knight who "in an evil hour . . . came into my house," which was true from the point of view of the poor inn's finances. But while the landlady is counting off her misfortunes, what does the Daughter do?

Thus the landlady went on in a great rage, and she was abetted by the worthy Maritornes. As for the daughter, she held her peace but now and then smiled. [P. 366]

Why does she not take sides with her mother in the legitimate defense of her interests? Why does she remain silent? Why did she smile "now and then"? The author does not tell us. And this is another one of the points where his silence speaks most eloquently. Now let us see—after another disappearance of the story— the final reappearance of this character. Keep in mind the incredible number of adventures that have taken place in the inn: first Don Quixote and Sancho, then Dorotea-Micomicona, later Doña Clara, and the rest. And now—with Don Quixote guarding the door of the "castle"—the entire house is quiet:

The only persons not asleep were the landlady's daughter and her maid, Maritornes. Since they both knew Don Quixote's weak points and that he was standing . . . outside, fully armed and on horseback, they resolved to play some tricks on him. [P. 442]

We should ask ourselves: what is this? What has happened? It seems quite normal to us that Maritornes, being who she is, should suggest some practical joke. But the Daughter too? That Daughter who is so fond of novels and has such compassion for knights? The author himself seems to have tentatively changed his

ideas about her. As a matter of fact, when he tells us
that they looked out of the hole in the loft, he fuses
them into one single category:

At this hole the two demimaidens took up their position
and saw Don Quixote on horseback, reclining on his lance
and heaving from time to time such deep and mournful
sighs that it seemed as if each one would tear his soul
asunder. [P. 442]

"Demimaidens"? Does that plural fuse one maiden
and a girl who is not maidenish—in a kind of arith-
metical mean? In other words, what has happened here
that Cervantes is hiding from us in this true history? Or
is it simply another oversight as it was in the case of
Sancho's burro? Since none of these is probably the real
explanation, and furthermore since that "demimaidens"
doesn't fit at all with the earlier description of the
Daughter, the following suggestion may clear up the
enigma: Cervantes is already thinking about what is
going to happen—not about what has happened—and
he is anticipating a moral judgment against the Daughter's honor. Be that as it may, the fact is that both demimaidens hear Don Quixote while he is delivering one of
his amorous oratories. "O my lady, Dulcinea . . . sum-
mit of all beauty . . ." The paragraph here takes up
nearly one entire column of the book. Are these eulogies to a lady not really a bit much, too much for the
ears of a girl who is indeed compassionate, but who is
also so fond of novels?

So far had Don Quixote proceeded in his mournful soliloquy
when the innkeeper's daughter softly called to him, whis-
pering: "Dear sir, come this way, if you please." [P. 443]

If we take into account the time and the place, no matter how innocent the child may be, this does not stop it from being real brazenness. Perhaps we will have to attribute it to the bad company of Maritornes. Perhaps. But let us turn our attention back to Don Quixote. Up to this moment we could well believe, because of his conduct, that he had renounced those double thoughts. But now the girl's pertness flusters him, and like any male under such circumstances, his heart —let us say—goes to his head. And instantly the "hole in the loft" turns into "a window with bars of gold":

At once he believed . . . that again, as once before, the beautiful damsel, daughter of the lord of the castle, conquered by love of him, had come to tempt him. [P. 443]

Does all this happen to a sexless creature? Next "he turned Rocinante about and came over to the hole." But at that moment, some idea must come into his head. Perhaps it is the double thoughts once more. If he remembers that again "as once before . . . [she] had come to tempt him," perhaps he also remembers what happened "once before." All this, combined with his status as an irreproachable knight, dictates his behavior—on principle.

I take pity on you, beauteous lady, because you have fixed your love where it is not possible for you to meet with the response. . . . Pardon me, therefore, good lady, and retire to your chamber and do not reveal your desires to me further, that I may not appear yet more ungrateful. [Pp. 443–444]

Notice that he begins by supposing that she calls him out of her desires, and that he opposes those with his own chastity and fidelity—but not asexual indifference.

But, if his words were to be taken literally, and if he were thinking only of Dulcinea, why all this? Besides being discourteous, it is cruel. Would it not have been better if he had pretended not to hear "whisperings" of any kind? But the fact is that deep within him, he continues to hope—as he did "once before." That such a thing happens shows us the little effort the demimaidens need to use in order to break down Don Quixote's delicate psychological balance. In fact, when the knight asks her about the Daughter, "What does she want?", Maritornes answers: "Only one of your hands." And then she leaves the hole and goes down to the stable for a halter at the same time that Don Quixote stands up on the saddle of his horse:

[so] that he might more easily reach the barred window at which he thought the love-sick damsel was standing. [P. 444]

And it is here that, like so many men, if not all of them, Don Quixote loses his head—for a woman—and he commits one of the few sins that Cervantes tells us about, as we are shown a frivolous and vain Don Quixote. Let us listen to what he says as he puts out his hand:

Take, lady, this hand, or as I should rather say, this lash of evildoers. Take this hand I say, which no other woman has ever touched, not even she herself who holds complete possession of my whole body. I give it to you, not that you may kiss it, but that you may behold the contexture of the sinews, the knitting of the muscles, the large and swelling veins. [P. 444]

But while he goes on, singing out his own praises—a warning for the vain—in spite of feeling the harshness of the rope that Maritornes is putting around his wrist, he does not realize that he has fallen into the noose (the halter), which his enamored vainglory has led him to. When Maritornes tied him up, "she and the other one, almost bursting with laughter"—left the knight in the most unstable balance in the world, not only because he was standing on his horse's saddle, hanging by one wrist to the hayloft window, but because now he feels unstable in the most precarious part of his vanity too. Could anything like this have happened to a sexless creature?

When some travelers arrive at the inn, the knight talks to them with an "arrogant voice." An arrogant voice, certainly, to compensate for the little arrogance of his material position and the much less arrogance of his internal position. As a result of all this, he falls, and remains hanging by an arm that is tied to the loft window—but he still goes on maintaining to the newcomers that the inn is a "castle." Now, *now*, less than ever can Don Quixote admit that it is not a castle and, therefore, enchanted, because if he did, we would only see a man, tied up by a coarse Asturian wench to the rail of a loft window.

Upon hearing Don Quixote's shouts, the innkeeper comes out. Maritornes, astutely, has untied the knight, and now we come to the important point. Don Quixote:

Without answering . . . slipped the halter from his wrist, and rising to his feet, he leaped on Rocinante, braced on his shield, couched his lance, and wheeling around the field, rode back at a half gallop, crying out: "Whoever shall dare to say that I have been justly enchanted . . . [P. 448]

Why does Don Quixote say "justly"? On none of the numerous occasions when Don Quixote has been enchanted does the knight say anything about whether it has been done justly or not. Why, then, does he do it now? Because, if I am not mistaken, Cervantes—in passing—wants to show us Don Quixote's feeling of guilt about his earlier frivolity.

Now let us look at the outcome of those earlier Quixotic loves. When they put the knight in the enchanted cart, the women of the inn go out to bid him farewell, and with them is the Daughter; and they pretend "to shed sorrowful tears at his misfortune." What does the knight say to this?

Do not weep, good ladies. . . . If these disasters did not befall me, I would not consider myself a famous knight-errant. [P. 472]

He recites his role again, but he adds:

Forgive me, fair ladies, if unwittingly I have given you any cause for annoyance, and pray to God that I may be delivered from the fetters. . . . If ever I am freed from them, never shall I forget to requite the favors you have bestowed upon me in this castle. [Pp. 472–473]

But what favors were those? And furthermore, what "annoyance" is Don Quixote referring to? Would it be going too far to interpret all this as a sublimation of the things that have happened to him at the inn, the driving force behind it certainly not being the "favors" they have given him, but the ones that the eyes of that very good looking lass seemed to promise? If the figure of the Daughter were to be considered an incidental character, how is it that she appears, disappears, and reappears so constantly? In my opinion, it is because that Daughter is Don Quixote's first real love. A love, of course, which does not and cannot affect the other one

—Dulcinea, to whom his status as a knight binds him —and he knows it.

To understand this better, we are now going to examine, comparatively, something that concerns Dulcinea herself. I am speaking of the fictitious novel invented by Sancho because of Don Quixote's letter. There comes a moment when Sancho summarizes, as follows, the message that he swears Dulcinea in person confided to him:

> and finally she told me . . . she was more eager to see you than to write to you. And she begged and commanded you on sight of this present to leave these thornbushes, give up your mad foolishness, and set out at once on the road to El Toboso . . . for she had mighty longing to see you. [P. 312]

What more could a love-sick knight desire in order to set out in search of his beloved? Did the Daughter have to beg him this much to make him give in? With her a "whisper" was enough. Let us look at this situation. Don Quixote limits himself to commenting with a great deal of frugality: "So far so good." How could it be any better when Dulcinea herself "begged and commanded you"—Sancho has invented no less than this—to go and see her? And with all this, Don Quixote spends his time on childish things like asking Sancho if he went there and back "through the air" so that he can finally ask his squire's advice about a point as important as this:

> But, to change the subject, what do you think I ought to do about my lady's order to go and see her? For although I perceive that I am bound to fulfill her behests, I find myself prevented by the boon I have granted to the princess. [P. 313]

Does Don Quixote's patience not seem suspicious? Having given his whole life to Dulcinea, at the moment when she begs and commands him to go and see her, he starts looking for excuses like a bad payer of debts. How should we interpret such strange conduct—especially in view of what happened with the Daughter? Don Quixote himself gives us the explanation very clearly:

On the one hand, my longing to see my lady disturbs and perplexes me; on the other, my plighted word and the glory I stand to reap in this enterprise incite and spur me on. [Pp. 313–314]

which is the same as saying—and clearly—that he does not want, nor does he intend, to go to El Toboso. It is from there, in fact, that the primary source of energy for all his understandings comes, but only so long as El Toboso remains off in the distance. We have already seen everything Don Quixote had to let Sancho do, when they were there, in order to get out of the village quickly. But now it happens that if he says this clearly, the game will be revealed; and so Don Quixote lies, he lies with all the candor of a small boy. And to find a solution for this heroic dilemma: love versus duty (no different from the Cid himself!), Don Quixote says:

What I intend to do is to travel by rapid stages and quickly get to the place where the giant is. Then, when I reach the place, I will cut off his head, install the princess . . . in her kingdom, and immediately return to the light that irradiates my senses; and I shall make such persuasive excuses that she shall even commend my delay. [P. 314]

Could he let his bad conscience be seen any more candidly? If his "Roman" sentiments about duty were so clear for him, why should he have to give such excuses? One who excuses himself, accuses himself. And furthermore, could his words be more childlike than they are? "I will go to the giant, I will cut off his head," and so on. That is, by lying, as Don Quixote lies here—because of it and not in spite of it—he shows himself to us much more as childlike, much more as having a pure soul . . . by that touch—"also ridiculous"—which only a pure soul, or a child, would know enough to add.

Altisidora

The sudden invasion of Altisidora into Don Quixote's life is rather brusque and puzzling. It happens when Don Quixote "felt an acute sense of loneliness" as we have seen. It is nighttime and hot, so the knight opens the window and hears a more or less pastoralized conversation between Emerencia and Altisidora. Don Quixote immediately preens himself:

He at once imagined that one of the duchess' maidens had fallen in love with him and that her modesty compelled her to keep her love a secret. He trembled at the thought that he might give in, but determined in his mind not to allow himself to be overcome. So, commending himself with heart and soul to his lady, Dulcinea of El Toboso, he resolved to listen to the music. And to let them know he was there, he pretended to sneeze. [P. 839]

Notice the inconstancy of his reasoning. On the one hand "he trembled at the thought that he might give in" to the fanciful temptation; but on the other hand, instead of closing himself in his room—out of sight, out of mind—he not only does not do this, but "he resolved to listen to the music," and to do it he pretends to sneeze so they will know he is present. What more could a psychoanalyst want, to see in the candid subterfuge of Don Quixote when he commends himself to his lady, the censorship that his conscious mind imposes on the subconscious?

At the sound of a harp, Altisidora begins to sing. And here Don Quixote undergoes another crisis of vanity, which only occurs—take note—when women go to his head:

Why am I so unhappy a knight that no damsel can gaze at me without falling in love? Why is the peerless Dulcinea so unlucky . . . ? [Pp. 841–842]

And now, in full swing, he soars:

Queens, what do you want from her? . . . Maidens of fifteen, why do you plague her? [P. 842]

And then, after asserting his incomparable fidelity:

With this he hastily closed the window and threw himself upon his bed, feeling as gloomy and out of sorts as if some misfortune had befallen him. [P. 842]

Why does he hastily close it now, and not before? Why does he feel "gloomy and out of sorts"? Could it be his hidden bad conscience? The History gives us some answer to these questions when the author, after remembering that he had left Don Quixote "rapt in the meditations aroused in him by the music of Altisidora," reveals to us:

No sooner did he go to bed with them [the meditations] than, like fleas, they plagued him, not letting him sleep a wink. [P. 850]

Is this not a clear explanation of that "he hastily closed the window" and especially the "gloomy and out of sorts" feeling? But finally morning comes. Don Quixote "flung the scarlet mantle over his shoulders and clapped on his head the green velvet cap." And after putting on his sword,

and picking up a large rosary, which he always carried with him, he strutted along with great pomp and solemnity toward the antechamber. [P. 850]

Only once before did the historian mention a rosary in connection with Don Quixote: that "rustic one" that he made himself at the time of his penance. Could it be the same one? Whatever the case, why was it not mentioned again until now? One might say that there had not been an opportunity before to mention such a detail. But there is the touch. Why does the author think that now is the time to do it? Because all night long Don Quixote had been gloomy and out of sorts thinking about Altisidora—and feeling guilty: that is why we have the show of religiosity, somewhat untimely under these circumstances.

So Don Quixote goes out, strutting; and when he passes through a gallery, there occurs Altisidora's spurious fainting scene, which I commented on previously. But if it was necessary only to mention it then, it seems that we must look at it more carefully now. First of all, in order to notice that Don Quixote, in spite of his rosary —a symbol of his good and chaste intentions—immediately softens in his resolution when faced with the feminine ploy:

Madam . . . I beseech you to order a lute to be left in my chamber this night, and I will console as best I can this

love-sick lady's grief. In these first blossomings of love
prompt undeceiving usually is an effective remedy. [P. 851]

In other words, Don Quixote "bites" here too—as we
see from his intentions to be consoling. But let us look
carefully: at first Don Quixote thinks about Dulcinea,
and furthermore he takes a rosary. Could we wish for a
more lucid double thought? But also just a few wom-
anly words are enough now to make the intention to
"console" arise in him. And are we supposed to see a
neuter, sexless creature in a gentleman like this?

As we will remember, the result of his consoling is
that "cat-clawing" which is the euphemism Don Quixote uses to tell about the "terrifying cat and bell scare"
that he mentions in his letter to Sancho. Don Quixote is
left scratched and bitten all over from the cat-clawing,
and Altisidora herself takes care of him "with her lily-
white hands," but not without throwing wood on the
fire with her spurious, "whispered" recriminations that
accuse him of "obstinacy and disdain." To this "Don
Quixote made no answer . . . but he sighed deeply."

It all costs him six days of being shut in and healing.
Until one night, "as he lay awake and watchful, brood-
ing over his misfortunes and over Altisidora's persecution," he hears someone tampering with the lock on his
door:

Immediately he imagined that the love-sick maiden was
coming to ambush his chastity and inveigle him into be-
traying the fidelity he owed to his lady, Dulcinea of El
Toboso. "No," he murmured . . . fully trusting his imagination, "the greatest beauty on earth shall not prevail upon
me to cease to adore . . . [P. 864]

Is it going too far to see evidence in these words of
something that is really almost the opposite of what

they say literally? Aside from this, the text itself almost says it to us point-blank. When Don Quixote gets to his feet, wrapped in his yellow satin quilt, he stares fixedly at the door and:

when he was hoping [1] to see the love-stricken and forlorn Altisidora come in, he saw a most venerable duenna. [P. 865]

Here he is: faithful, chaste, calling on Dulcinea's name, but the fact is that his own historian swears that "he was hoping to see the love-stricken Altisidora come in."

The entire scene with Doña Rodríguez and Don Quixote follows, both of them having scruples, and both asking for reciprocal guarantees: but Don Quixote does not give up even then. To begin with, he asks Doña Rodríguez, "Do you come to me on an errand of mediation and love?" Who is it that might have been able to use the Rodríguez woman as an intermediary, in Don Quixote's mind? As it will be remembered, after the duenna's gossiping, the scene ends with the pinchings and slapping that the "enchanters" deal first to her and then to him. With Don Quixote:

pulling off his sheet and quilt, they pinched him so hard and so often that he was compelled to defend himself with his fists, and all this in an admirable silence. [P. 871]

Admirable, indeed: like almost all the silences in this book. How is it that here Don Quixote does not utter any paragraph at all, or call on the name Dulcinea or the heroes of his books? Simply because he knows. And so he does not speak, but merely defends himself "in an admirable silence."

[1] esperaba (Trans. note.)

The thread of his loves disappears and reappears at different times here too. The first reappearance is when Don Quixote leaves the castle. I am referring to Altisidora's accusation—that her garters were stolen—a scene which has been commented on previously. So I will note now that Don Quixote does not give up the thought that the girl is in love with him, which means that he does not give up thinking that he is capable of making her fall in love:

This maid speaks, as she admits, like one love-sick, for which I am not to blame. And so I have no reason to ask pardon of her or of your excellency. [P. 934]

And he leaves the castle, in full possession of his dignity, but convinced that Altisidora is in love with him. For this reason, when he found himself in the open country:

safe and sound and free from Altisidora's endearments, he fancied himself in his own element. [P. 935]

And it is at this time that he intones his hymn to liberty, as I have pointed out elsewhere. But as to whether he really was or was not in his own element, "free from Altisidora's endearments," is another matter. In the same chapter there begin the traces of melancholy. It is here that he utters his famous words, "I do not know what I conquer by force of my labor," and then he enigmatically adds:

But should my Dulcinea [be disenchanted] . . . and my mind set aright, who knows but I may direct my steps along a better road than that which I am now following. [P. 937]

As we see, the hymn to liberty ends with a sound that is more like a dirge than a song. But since Sancho changes the topic of conversation to Altisidora, Don Quixote asserts that love strikes the great as well as the humble, making them all shameless:

So, Altisidora, being shameless, proclaimed her desires, which roused in my heart more confusion than compassion. [P. 939]

But such gentle words are negated almost immediately, when they fall into "the nets of shepherds":

May I die if the enchanters who persecute me do not want to entangle me in them [the nets] . . . as if in vengeance for my cruelty to Altisidora! [P. 940]

Did he not just say that Altisidora's desires aroused in his heart "more confusion than compassion"? Did the historian not state that when Don Quixote found himself free from Altisidora's endearments "he felt he was in his own element"? And yet, two or three pages later we find out that Don Quixote accuses himself of being "cruel" to the girl. Would it be too much to see in this feeling of guilt, the first pang of anguish, nostalgia, loneliness? But loneliness or nostalgia for what?—or for whom? For Dulcinea?

Altisidora once more disappears from the story until the master and servant come upon Roque Guinart (the "generous bandit") who orders his men to give back to Sancho what they have taken from him. And then Roque asks Sancho if everything is all right, and the squire answers yes, "but that three handkerchiefs were missing, worth three cities." And when one of the villains is amazed at Sancho's exaggerated words, it is not he but his master who answers, in a most unexpected way—apparently:

my squire values them at the price he mentioned for the sake of the person who gave them to me. [P. 962]

And so we realize that without Don Quixote's wanting to—but with the wishes of Cervantes—the knight still had not forgotten the endearments that seemed to bother him so much, according to the voice of his chaste conscience, but had come to take on such meaning for him that he subscribes to Sancho's exaggerated words: for the sake of the person who gave them. Notice, by the way, the construction of the phrase: "my squire values them for the sake of the person who gave them to me"—and not, for example, for the sake of the person who gave them to him.

We have an eclipse of Altisidora again, and then another appearance. In order to orient the reader to this situation, I will say that it is at the time when we have the transformation of the knight conquered by Don Quixote, into a simple lackey of the Duke: Tosilos. Don Quixote asks Sancho:

But tell me now, did you ask that Tosilos, as you call him, what has been the fate of Altisidora; whether she has wept for my absence, or already cast into oblivion those amorous desires that tormented her in my presence? [P. 1004]

In any case, he has not "cast into oblivion" the flattering remarks that bothered him so much. But when Sancho says that that was not the time "to ask such foolish questions," Don Quixote brings things to a head:

Look here, Sancho . . . there is a great deal of difference between acts that are done out of love and those done out of gratitude. A knight may well not be in love, but strictly speaking, he must never be ungrateful. Altisidora, to all appearances, loved me deeply; she gave me the three kerchiefs you know of; she wept at my departure; she cursed me; she abused me; and in spite of shame, she complained of me publicly—all certain proofs that she adored me. [Pp. 1004–1005]

A tirade, in paragraphs, about his incomparable fidelity to Dulcinea follows, which, delivered at that moment, makes it significant. Furthermore, if he was so lost in thought about Dulcinea, why does it occur to him to ask about Altisidora?

Let us look at the end of this second love. Now defeated, Don Quixote once more approaches the Duke's castle: it is the "death" of Altisidora, whose "resurrection" depends on Sancho. Finally, when the girl shows signs of reviving, Don Quixote does not react this time as we would have expected in view of everything that has happened, which we have tried to summarize, but:

When Don Quixote saw Altisidora begin to move, he went and knelt before Sancho, saying: "Now is the time, son of my loins . . . to give yourself some of those lashes to which you are pledged for disenchanting Dulcinea." [P. 1019]

How is it that here Don Quixote, who esteemed so highly the girl's handkerchiefs, does not show any emotion when he sees no less than her "resurrection," but instead, now remembers Dulcinea? Let us leave the answer—supposing that it is correct—for later, and notice only that the historian tells us nothing about Don Quixote, but does talk about Altisidora. She, "pretending to be faint" and "looking across at Don Quixote," said to him:

God forgive you, loveless knight; because of your cruelty
I have been . . . in the other world. [P. 1020]

We are made to wait for the first Quixotic declaration about such supernatural abuse until nighttime,
when Don Quixote and Sancho are alone. The first
asks:

What do you think, Sancho, of this evening's adventure?
Great and powerful are the powers of love scorned, and
with your own eyes you have seen Altisidora dead, slain by
no other arrows . . . [P. 1021]

Are we not back in the presence of Don Quixote's
magic recourses to continue what we have been calling
his game? But, supposing that this is so, how should we
interpret it now? For me, there is no doubt: Don Quixote knows. And because he knows that he is indeed
dealing with enchantment—not of his own, however,
but that of the castle of the Duke and Duchess—he, of
course, speaks in paragraphs about the miracle, so that
he would not undermine his role as a knight. But: the
moment has arrived for us to remember Don Quixote's
letter to Sancho, telling him about his decision to leave
the castle. Because then, as now, I think that what occurs is simply that Don Quixote sees through the Duke
and Duchess. Let us see. This time Altisidora—not Doña
Rodríguez—presents herself in Don Quixote's room.
And not in any ordinary way, but:

crowned with the same garment she had worn on the tomb,
and clad in a tunic of white taffeta flowered with gold, her
hair loose upon her shoulders, leaning on a black staff of
finest ebony. [P. 1023]

But this time Don Quixote was not hoping to see her,
nor are we told that he felt as if he were on a bed of

hot coals in one of his "crazy" fantasies. Nonetheless, does this not seem to be the most opportune time for it? Does Don Quixote not seem to be convinced of this "death from love," as well as the "resurrection?" And yet, let us see:

At her presence [Altisidora's] Don Quixote, troubled and abashed, shrank down and completely covered himself under the sheets and quilts of his bed, dumbfounded and unable to utter a single word of greeting. [P. 1023]

Why? Why does Don Quixote, normally so courteous, at a time when he might seem to be at such a "climactic" moment (to people who like such a word), remain mute? Because now he knows; because everything has confirmed his premonitory fears—double thoughts—which caused him to leave the castle. And so, even when Altisidora recites all her memorized role of amorous recriminations, Don Quixote remains harder than marble to her complaints. And when Altisidora wants to take up her amorous complaints again, the knight interrupts her:

I have told you many times, madam, how distressed I am that you should fix your affections on me . . . I was born to belong to Dulcinea . . . and to think that any other beauty can occupy the place she holds in my heart is to imagine the impossible. [P. 1025]

These are words that state better than any others that it is too late for such things, and as far as enchantments are concerned, he will stick with his own: "Dulcinea." Because now there is no doubt: the knight is really aggravated. Or have we forgotten the knight's very soft words to Maritornes-Daughter? Why all this? Because now he definitely knows: he knows what is happening in this castle, he knows who the mocking, though discreet, Altisidora is. And so he answers with that dryness—unimaginable at the beginning when he wanted "to console her" or, even later, when he contritely remembered the girl's endearments.

The words of Altisidora herself are a reflection of this dryness:

My God, Don Codfish . . . I'll tear your eyes out if I can get at you! Do you really imagine, Don Vanquished, Don Cudgeled, that I died for you? All you've seen tonight has been pretense. [Pp. 1025–1026]

words that are not only furious, but inflamed too, when she reminds him of what she knows will be a burning point: "Don Vanquished, Don Cudgeled." Nevertheless, Don Quixote says nothing to such ill-intended words. But when the Duke and Duchess finally appear:

Don Quixote begged them for leave to depart that same day, since it was more fitting for a vanquished knight like himself to live in a pigsty than in a royal palace. [P. 1026]

These are painful words that prove that those others, the words of Altisidora, have wounded him to the quick. The Duke and Duchess grant him their leave, but when they ask him if Altisidora still remains in his good graces, Don Quixote puts an end to this romance with the following words:

Madam . . . your ladyship should know that this damsel's malady proceeds from idleness. The remedy for that is honest and continuous occupation. She has just informed me that they wear lace in hell, and since she must certainly know how to make it, let it never be out of her hands. When she is busily working her bobbins, the image or images of her desires will not work in her imagination. That is the truth, and that is my . . . advice. [Pp. 1026–1027]

There it is, pure and simple. Is it not a bit excessive? Is there not too great a contrast between the beginning and end of this romance? How should we interpret this? I would say that now Don Quixote is wounded in his soul: in his pure-beautiful soul itself. First he knows he is conquered; and then, he *knows:* the mockery, the masquerade of everything that touches the castle and its Duke and Duchess. So it is not too much for him to speak ill of those who have offended him.

After this moment, Don Quixote never again mentions the name of Altisidora. So this romance ends here, and as we see, it is one of those that "have an unhappy ending." After this, Don Quixote understands: too much. And now he does not even find an inner refuge in Dulcinea. In other words: for the first time perhaps, he sees there is something that at the last moment, at the moment of truth, we cannot avoid, even with games.

Just a few more lines about this point. After what we have seen, I do not think that we can continue to speak of Don Quixote as "sexless." And so, I would say, we cannot apply this term to Myshkin either. Both of them, being men, feel attracted by women—and not by merely one woman either. And in this aspect, even though Don Quixote's reactions—his preenings—seem more significant than those of Myshkin, I do not think Don Quixote's double thoughts can be ignored without deforming his entire personality by that omission. Whatever the case, the conduct of both men when they are with women seems to me perfectly clear (I am thinking of Gide's idea about the possible impotence of Myshkin) inasmuch as the word, the simple word "chastity," does not seem like an insignificant term at all. When all is said and done, is the conduct of both these "poor knights" so anomalous, if we think about the state of their pure-beautiful souls?

Let us leave the final word on this matter to Tom Sawyer. As a real child, perhaps he may explain what evidently seems to be inexplicable:

"Say, Becky, was you ever engaged?"

"What's that?"

"Why, engaged to be married."

"No."

"Would you like to?"

"I reckon so. I don't know. What is it like?"

"Like? Why it ain't like anything. You only just tell a boy you won't ever have anybody but him, ever ever *ever*, and then you kiss and that's all. Anybody can do it."

"Kiss? What do you kiss for?"

"Why, that, you know, is to—well, they always do that."

. . . She resisted, for a while, and then said:

"You turn your face away so you can't see, and then I will. But you mustn't ever tell anybody—*will* you, Tom? Now you won't, *will* you?"

"No, indeed, indeed I won't. Now, Becky."

He turned his face away. She bent timidly around till her breath stirred his curls and whispered, "I—love—you!" . . .

"Now, Becky, it's all done—all over but the kiss. Don't you be afraid of that—it ain't anything at all. Please, Becky." And he tugged at her apron and the hands.

By and by she gave up, and let her hands drop; her face, all glowing with the struggle, came up and submitted. Tom kissed the red lips . . . [Pp. 62–63]

Would we say that this is lust? But on the other hand, does it show something asexual—sexless?

6

The Moment of Truth

Everything that I have been proposing in these pages finds its confirmation in the text, and clearly, from the moment that Don Quixote leaves the enchanted castle. The historian tells us that Don Quixote was feeling sad because he had been defeated, but was very happy to have seen Sancho's magic powers as evidenced by Altisidora's resurrection. But he establishes a scruple that could not be more essential for my viewpoint:

although he was somewhat reluctant to believe that the lovelorn maiden had really died. [P. 1028]

Now it is not I, but the author of the book, who tells us like this, as if in passing, that Don Quixote knows. Let us look at some other cases. Regarding the disenchantment of Dulcinea, Sancho makes what we might call a business proposal, which his master immediately accepts. After the deal is made—so much money per lashing—Don Quixote says some other words that are also very significant:

O blessed Sancho! . . . How solemnly shall we be bound, Dulcinea and I, to serve you, all the days that Heaven shall grant us. If she returns to her former self, as she must, her misfortune will turn to good fortune. [Pp. 1029–1030]

Do we not have to see in these words—along with the scruple about Altisidora's death—a real disenchantment? And not of Dulcinea, but of Don Quixote—a disenchanted Don Quixote, who continues to profess, certainly, but now without any conviction at all? Now the game has lost whatever it had of magic; and, reduced to a mere game, we see how Don Quixote reconciles himself to playing by commitment, perhaps so that he will not disappoint Sancho. But it happens that the latter, shortly afterward, carried away by his enthusiasm —although he thinks it is his "business deal"—retires to some beech trees to lash himself with his burro's halter, made into a whip. But:

When Don Quixote saw him go off so briskly and resolutely, he remarked: "Mind you do not lash yourself to pieces; give time for one stroke to await another . . . I mean, do not lay on so fiercely that you might kill yourself before reaching the required number." [P. 1030]

Don Quixote does not doubt for one instant the resolution and briskness with which his squire will whip himself; and so, because he knows, he feels guilty and cannot allow the games to go to extremes:

Heaven forbid, friend Sancho, that you should lose your life for my pleasure, for it must help to support your wife and children. Let Dulcinea wait until a more auspicious

occasion presents itself, and I shall live in hopes that when you have regained new strength . . . [P. 1031]

We are confronted with words that should be questioned: in the first place, why does he prefer to say "my pleasure" instead of what should be Dulcinea's life? In addition, how could Don Quixote offer such blasphemy: "Let Dulcinea wait until a more auspicious occasion presents itself."? But if we accept the idea that he knows the truth about Dulcinea's existence—"God knows whether she is fantastical or not"—then it is clear that "Dulcinea can wait," but his friend's back, which he believes is really being martyred (and for my "pleasure"), cannot. Because he is a pure soul this is impossible for him.

Now we are coming to their arrival at the village. Sancho, now "literary," falls to his knees and utters a paragraph worthy of his master's best moments:

Open your eyes, beloved home of mine, and behold your son Sancho Panza come back again, if not very rich, at least very well whipped. Open your arms and welcome your son Don Quixote too, who, though he was conquered by another, nevertheless conquered himself. [P. 1038]

What does Don Quixote say upon hearing his own words (for, in a way, they could not be more his own)? Will he go back into the game again? Does he assent, at least tacitly?

"A truce to your foolish prattle," said Don Quixote, "and let us step with our right foot foremost as we enter our native village, where we shall give our imaginations play and lay down the plans for our intended pastoral life." [P. 1038]

If there is a sentence that, in itself, carries a complete stamp—"Made by Cervantes"—this is it beyond any shadow of a doubt. When he listens to Sancho at first, and hears his own voice, he cannot constrain himself, and he explodes; for, when he feels "outside" the game, he sees the insanity of it all: "a truce to your foolish prattle." But on the other hand, realizing that he has gone too far, he leaves the door open, as the saying goes, perhaps out of compassion for Sancho when he sees him so unbelievably won over to his own cause: "lay down the plans for our intended pastoral life."

As they enter the village the "auguries" appear ("*Malum signum, malum signum. A hare runs away, hounds pursue her, and Dulcinea does not appear.*") In spite of these, we are still to see that sort of final flaming of enthusiast virtue, when Don Quixote tells the Curate and the Bachelor about his pastoral plans. But the fire does not burn again. Now, when the Housekeeper and the Niece argue with him, opposing the new plans, Don Quixote here pronounces the final words:

My dear girls, do cease your prating . . . I know best what I have to do; only help me to my bed, for I do not feel very well. Remember that whether I be a knight-errant or an errant shepherd, you will always find me ready to provide for you. [P. 1043]

This is the last time that he speaks "in code." He feels that his life is ending. The doctor verifies the fact. The knight, as we know, sleeps for six hours, and then he is another man. And when they ask him, he answers:

My judgement is now clear and unfettered. . . . I find, dear niece, that my end approaches, but I would have it remembered that though in my life I was reputed a madman, yet in my death this opinion was not confirmed. Therefore, my dear child, call my good friends, the priest, the bachelor Sansón Carrasco . . . for I wish to make my confession and my will. [P. 1045]

He receives the friends with the very famous words:

I am no longer Don Quixote of La Mancha, but Alonso Quixano, the man whom the world formerly called the Good, owing to his virtuous life. I am now the sworn enemy of Amadis. [P. 1045]

Called the "Good," of course. But "Good" alone? To understand this more fully, let us look at Don Quixote's testament that has, for our purpose, a definitive importance. The notary is now at his bedside, and Don Quixote, "when he came to the legacies," said:

Item, I give and bequeath to Sancho Panza, whom in my madness I made my squire, whatever money he has of mine in his possession; and whereas there are accounts and reckonings to be settled between us for what he has received and disbursed, my will and pleasure is that he should not be required to furnish any account of such sums . . . for his honesty and his faithfulness deserve it. [P. 1047]

Notice that these are words from someone who knows he is dying. And even yet, the knight who "is now the sworn enemy of Amadis," who has confessed and is prepared to die as God wills, does not resist making a final wink with that "item," fully intelligible only to Sancho (and, thanks to Cervantes, to us too, of course). Showing that the knight is faithful until death—just that: to the game, to the magic of the game, even when it is over.

And with this, we shall let the knight rest in peace.

What significance does or could all this realism, all this sanity have, which is so manifest in the final chapters of the book? In a way, they are signs of maturity: the maturity of this "child" which I have been proposing. But since Don Quixote is not a real child, here it is the true maturity of ripe fruit: ripe to fall and to come to an end, as ripe fruit must. And so we have Don Quixote's trimming of sails: for the ripeness of life is death, and one does not play with death. That is why Don Quixote seems to turn his back on Don Juan —his carnal cousin. To the latter's "how long you give me to live," [1] the pure soul of Don Quixote seems to answer "how long you have given me to live."

So it does not seem to me that Don Quixote "dies from sadness at seeing the world so inferior to him" as Menéndez Pidal suggests. But rather the contrary: he feels a sadness, an incurable sadness, because now too, he knows: he knows that with death, there are no games that matter.

Nor can I agree with Turkevich's opinion on this point when she suggests:

When don Quixote is deprived of his mania, he sinks into apathy. . . . So long as Myshkin had his concept of beauty, he lived and worked for it, but when Nastasya Filipovna's flight and death wrench it from him, he becomes permanently deranged—equivalent, for him, to death. [Pp. 129–130]

Even if these words can be applied to Myshkin, and in a way we cannot deny the fact, given Dostoevski's dénouement, to me they do not seem valid for Don Quixote. In this case, too, it would be quite the con-

---

[1] "tan largo me lo fiáis" (Trans. note.)

trary: insofar as Don Quixote sinks into apathy—the apathy of death—he feels "deprived of his mania"; or he renounces his game.

His will and his "legacy" to Sancho seem to me a greater proof. Don Quixote, being sane now, still does not forget about his previous madness. That wink, that allusion to certain "received and disbursed" things, constitutes the secret sign that unites sanity and "magic" on the one hand, and on the other, at the moment of truth, annuls the entire game.

Bibliography

Alonso, Dámaso. *Del siglo de oro a este siglo de siglos* (Sancho-Quijote; Sancho-Sancho, pp. 9–20). Madrid: Ed. Gredos, 1962.

Castro, Américo. *El pensamiento de Cervantes. Revista de filología española.* Anejo 6. Madrid, 1925.

——. *Hacia Cervantes.* Madrid: Ed. Taurus, 1960.

——. *Semblanzas y estudios literarios.* Princeton: Princeton University Press, 1956.

Cervantes, Miguel de. *Don Quixote of La Mancha.* Trans. Walter Starkie. New York: New American Library, 1964.

Clemens, Samuel. (See Twain, Mark)

Clemens, Cyril. *Young Sam Clemens.* Ed. Leon Tebbetts. Portland, Me., 1942.

De Voto, Bernard A. *Mark Twain at Work.* "Boy's Manuscript" is a sketch by Mark Twain from which his *Tom Sawyer* was subsequently developed. Cambridge, Mass.: Harvard University Press, 1942.

Dostoyevsky, Fyodor. *The Idiot.* Trans. Constance Garnett. New York: Dell Publishing Co., 1962.

Gide, André. *Dostoievsky.* Paris: Ed. Henri Jonquières et Co., 1928.

Gilman, Stephen. "Cervantes en la obra de Mark Twain." *Cuadernos de Insula,* I, 204–222. Madrid, 1947.

Giusti, Wolfango L. "Sul 'donchisciottismo' di alcuni personaggi del Dostohevskij." *Cultura.* Roma-Ginebra (Feb., 1931), pp. 171–179.

Grismer, Raymond L. *Cervantes: a bibliography.* New York: H. W. Wilson Co., 1946.

———.*Cervantes: a Bibliography.* Vol. II. Minneapolis: Brigges-Beckwith, 1963.

Hazard, Paul. *Don Quichotte de Cervantes.* Paris: E. Mellotée, 1932.

Krieger, Murray. *The Tragic Vision.* New York: Holt, Reinhart and Winston, 1960 (The part pertaining to *The Idiot* is entitled: "The Curse of Saintliness").

Madariaga, Salvador. *Guía del lector del Quijote.* Buenos Aires: Ed. Sudamericana, 1943.

Malkiel, Yakov. "Cervantes in Nineteenth-Century Russia." *Comparative Literature.* Vol. III. University of Oregon, Eugene, Oregon, 1951, pp. 310–329.

Menéndez Pidal, Ramón. *España y su historia* (Un aspecto en la elaboración del Quijote. Cervantes y el ideal caballeresco). Tomo II. Madrid: Ed. Minotauro, 1957. Pp. 178–234.

Merejkowski, D. de. "Cervantes." *Hispania.* IV (Paris, 1921), 97–124.

Moore, Olin Harris. "Mark Twain and Don Quixote." *PMLA,* XXXVII, (1922), 324–346.

Ortega y Gasset, José. *Obras* (Meditaciones del Quijote e ideas sobre la novela. Meditación de El Escorial). Madrid-Barcelona: Espasa-Calpe, 1932.

Paine, Albert Bigelow. *Mark Twain's Notebook* prepared for publication with comments by Albert Bigelow Paine. New York: Harper and Brothers, 1935.

Salinas, Pedro. *Ensayos de literatura hispánica.* Madrid: Ed. Aguilar, 1958.

Twain, Mark. *The Adventures of Tom Sawyer and The Adventures of Huckleberry Finn.* New York: The Modern Library, 1940.

Turgenev, Ivan. *Hamlet and Don Quijote.* Ed. M. J. Bernardete and Angel Flores. Ithaca, N.Y.: The Dragon Press, 1932. Pp. 98–120.

Turkevich, Ludmilla B. "Cervantes in Russia:" in *Cervantes Across the Centuries.* A quadricentennial volume edited by Angel Flores and M. J. Bernardete. New York: Dryden Press, 1947. Pp. 343–371.

———. *Cervantes in Russia*. Princeton: Princeton University Press, 1950.

Unamuno, Miguel de. *Vida de don Quijote y Sancho*. Ed. Espasa-Calpe. Col. Austral, Vol. 33. Madrid-Buenos Aires, 1958.

Wellek, René. *Dostoyevsky. A Collection of Critical Essays*. Englewood Cliffs, N. J.: Prentice-Hall, 1965.

I am including below two other works that I was not able to consult since they have not been translated into any language I know. I have seen references to Bem in the works of Turkevich and Malkiel, and to Prohaska in Giusti's work. The two works below are not listed in the *Library of Congress Catalog of Printed Cards*, the *Library of Congress Author Catalog*, or in the *Library of Congress National Union Catalog*.

Bem, A. L. *U istokov tvochestva Dostoyevskago* [A source of Dostoevski's works]. Prague, 1936.

Prohaska, ? (Giusti does not give the author's first name) *Dostoyevskij. Studija u sveslavenskom covjeku*. Zagabria, 1921.